Gay Men, Lesbians, and the Law

Gay Men, Lesbians, and the Law

RUTHANN ROBSON

MARTIN DUBERMAN
General Editor

CHELSEA HOUSE PUBLISHERS
New York ■ Philadelphia

CHELSEA HOUSE PUBLISHERS

EDITORIAL DIRECTOR   Richard Rennert
EXECUTIVE MANAGING EDITOR   Karyn Gullen Browne
COPY CHIEF   Robin James
PICTURE EDITOR   Adrian G. Allen
CREATIVE DIRECTOR   Robert Mitchell
ART DIRECTOR   Joan Ferrigno
PRODUCTION MANAGER   Sallye Scott

ISSUES IN LESBIAN AND GAY LIFE
SENIOR EDITOR   Sean Dolan
SERIES DESIGN   Basia Niemczyc

Staff for GAY MEN, LESBIANS, AND THE LAW
ASSISTANT EDITOR   Annie McDonnell
PICTURE RESEARCHER   Toby Greenberg

Introduction © 1994 by Martin B. Duberman.

First Printing

1 3 5 7 9 8 6 4 2

Library of Congress Cataloging-in-Publication Data

Robson, Ruthann, 1956–
Gay men, lesbians, and the law/Ruthann Robson.
p. cm.—(Issues in lesbian and gay life)
Includes bibliographical references and index.
Summary: Discusses the legal aspects of homosexuality in such areas as discrimination,
education, and health.
ISBN 0-7910-2612-4
      0-7910-2963-8 (pbk.)
1. Homosexuality—Law and legislation—United States—Juvenile literature. 2. Lesbians—Legal status, laws, etc.—United States—Juvenile literature. 3. Gay men—Legal
status, laws, etc.—United States—Juvenile literature. [1. Homosexuality—Law and
legislation.] I. Title. II. Series.
KF4754.5.Z9R63 1995   95-6668
346.7301'3—dc20   CIP
[347.30613]   AC

FRONTISPIECE: A variety of individual and societal attitudes toward
homosexuality are reflected in this photograph taken of Queer Nation's
"kiss-in" in San Francisco in 1994.

◼ *Contents* ◼

◼ *Issues in Lesbian and Gay Life* ◼

Other titles in preparation

How Different?

MARTIN DUBERMAN

Just how different *are* gay people from heterosexuals? Different enough to support the common notion that they form a subculture—a shared set of group attitudes, behaviors and institutions that set them distinctively apart from mainstream culture? Of course the notion of the "mainstream" is itself difficult to define, given the many variations in religion, region, class, race, age and gender that in fact make up what we call "the heartland." And the problems of definition are further confounded when we broaden the discussion—as we should—from the context of the United States to a global one.

The question of the extent of "differentness"—of "queerness"—is subject to much debate, within as well as without the lesbian and gay world, and there are no easy answers for it. On one level, of course, all human beings share commonalities that revolve around basic needs for nurturance, affiliation, support and love, and those commonalities are so profound that they dwarf the cultural differences that set people apart.

Besides, it often isn't clear precisely what differences are under scrutiny. If we confine the discussion to erotic and affectional preference, then gay people are obviously different because of their primary attraction to members of their own gender. But what more, if anything, follows from that? Gay conservatives tend to believe that nothing follows, that aside from the matter of erotic orientation, gay people are "just folks"—just like everyone else.

But gay radicals tend to dispute that. They insist gay people have had a special history and that it has induced a special way of looking at the world. The radicals further insist that those middle-class gay white men who *deny* that their experience has been unusual enough to differentiate them from the mainstream are suffering from "false consciousness"—that they *are* more different—out of bed, as well as in—than they themselves would like to admit.

If one asked the average person what it is that sets gay men and lesbians apart, the likely answer would be that gay men are "effeminate" and lesbians "butch." Which is another way of saying that they are not "real" men or "real" women—that is, that they do not conform to prescribed cultural norms in regard to gender. It is true, historically, that "fairies" and "dykes" *have* been the most visible kind of gay person (perhaps because they were unable to "pass"), and over time they became equated in the popular mind with *all* gay people.

Yet even today, when gay men are often macho-looking body-builders and "lipstick" lesbians playfully flaunt their stereotypically feminine wiles, it can still be argued that gay people—whatever behavioral style they may currently adopt—are, irreducibly, gender nonconformists. Beneath many a muscled gay body still lies an atypically gentle, sensitive man; beneath the makeup and the skirts often lies an unusually strong, assertive woman.

This challenge to conventional gender norms—a self-conscious repudiation on the part of lesbian/gay radicals—is not a minor thing. And the challenge is compounded by the different kinds of relationships and families gay people form. A typical gay male or lesbian couple does *not* divide up chores, attitudes, or desire according to standard bi-polar "husband" and "wife" roles. Gay couples are usually two-career households in which an egalitarian sharing of rights and responsibilities remains the ideal, and often even the practice. And more and more gay people (particularly lesbians) are making the decision to have and raise children—children who are not trained to look to daddy for discipline and mommy for emotional support.

All this said, it remains difficult to *specify* the off-center cultural attitudes and variant institutional arrangements of lesbian and gay life. For one thing, the gay world is an extremely diverse one. It is not at all clear how much a black lesbian living in a small southern town has in common with a wealthy gay male advertising executive in New York City—or a transgendered person with either.

Perhaps an analogy is useful here. Literary critics commonly and confidently refer to "the Jewish novel" as a distinctive genre of writing. Yet when challenged to state *precisely* what special properties set such a novel apart from, say, a book by John Updike, the critics usually fall back on vague, catchall distinctions—like characterizing a "Jewish" novel as one imbued with "a kind of serious, kvetschy, doom-ridden humor."

Just so with any effort to compile an exact, comprehensive listing of the ways in which gay and lesbian subcultures (and we must always keep in mind that they are multiple, and sometimes at odds) differ from mainstream patterns. One wag summed up the endless debate this way: "No, there is no such thing as a gay subculture. And yes, it has had an enormous influence on mainstream life." Sometimes, in other words, one can *sense* the presence of the unfamiliar or offbeat without being able fully to articulate its properties.

Even if we could reach agreement on whether gay male and lesbian culture(s) stand marginally or profoundly apart from the mainstream, we would then have to account for those differences. Do they result from strategies adapted over time to cope with oppression and ghettoization? Or are they centrally derived from some intrinsic, biological subset—a "gay gene," for example, which initially creates an unconventional kind of person who then, banding together with likeminded others, create a novel set of institutional arrangements?

This interlocking series of books, *Issues in Lesbian and Gay Life,* is designed to explore the actual extent of "differentness" from mainstream values and institutions. It presents detailed discussions on a wide range of gay and lesbian experience and expression—from marriage and parenting, to history and politics, to spirituality and theology. The aim is to provide the reader with enough detailed, accurate information so that he or she can come to their own conclusions as to whether or not lesbian and gay subculture(s) represent, taken in their entirety, a significant departure from mainstream norms.

Whatever one concludes, one should always remember that differentness is not a disability nor a deficiency. It is another way, not a lesser way. Indeed, alternate styles of seeing (and being) can breathe vital new life into traditional forms that may have rigidified over time. Variant perspectives and insights can serve all at once to highlight the narrowness of conventional mores—*and* present options for broadening and re-vivifying their boundaries.

❖   ❖   ❖

Ruthann Robson's *Gay Men, Lesbians, and the Law* provides a detailed, comprehensive guide to the many ways—the changing ways—in which judicial opinion and legislative statute affect the daily lives of lesbians, gay men, bisexuals, and transgendered people.

The influence of the law over our lives is profound. On a practical level, it determines such central matters as education, military service, spousal rights, insurance coverage, the legality of wills, and the legitimacy of family structures. On a symbolic level, legal decisions as to what is or is not "acceptable" behavior has a far-reaching effect on forming the attitudes of the public at large towards lesbians and gay men.

Historically, the law has been hostile to the rights—even to the existence—of same-gender love and lust. And as a result of negative judicial opinions and legislative statutes, lesbians and gay men have, through time, suffered enormities of discrimination.

Robson describes this history, but goes beyond it to assess recent changes in the law and, as well, to provide a thorough analysis of the varied strategies available for accelerating the pace of change. Her skillful, succinct coverage of a large number of topics makes *Gay Men, Lesbians, and the Law* an invaluable and accessible guide through the intricate corridors of the legal world.

Introduction

RUTHANN ROBSON

The law influences the everyday lives of lesbians, gay men, bisexuals, and transgendered people in a practical way. The law may determine whether or not one will be arrested for certain sexual activity, whether or not one will be discriminated against, or whether or not one will have one's intimate relationships respected. The law also has tremendous influence over social attitudes, influencing lives in a more symbolic and indirect way. Changes in the law have affected opinions about the acceptability of sexual diversity, the opinions of lesbians, gay men, bisexuals, and transgendered people included.

These changes have often occurred because a few lesbians, gay men, bisexuals, and transgendered people took tremendous risks. Attempts to change the law can take several forms. One form is legislative: lobbying Congress, state legislatures, or local councils for changes in statutes or ordinances. Another form is litigation: either defending or bringing an action in court. Still another form is administrative: arguing in proceedings brought either by or against agencies of federal, state, or local governments. In all of these forms, the people involved sometimes endure extreme stress, expense, and disruption of their lives. They also risk making the situation worse. There is never any guarantee that an encounter with the legal system will have a positive outcome.

Whether an outcome is negative or positive, it can affect many more people than those directly involved in the attempt to change the law.

In the case of legislative change, a statute or ordinance applies to every person within the jurisdiction. For example, if the state of Iowa adopts a law that prohibits discrimination against lesbians and gay men, that law applies to everyone in the state. With litigation, a case may set precedent for other cases in the same jurisdiction depending upon the level of the court that decided it. These levels follow the pattern of a pyramid, with many trial courts, fewer appellate courts, and one high court. For example, if a trial judge in Maryland decides that a high school may not exclude lesbian couples from attending the prom, other trial judges in Maryland are not bound by the decision. The high school could also appeal this decision to the appropriate appellate court in Maryland, which could either affirm or reverse. This appellate decision would be precedent for all the trial courts within its jurisdiction, but only persuasive authority for all the trial courts within the jurisdiction of other appellate courts. However, the appellate decision could also be appealed to the state's highest court, usually but not always known as the supreme court. The decision of the state's highest court is precedent for all the other courts within the state. A trial court or appellate court must follow the decision of the state's highest court, even if the lower courts disagree. Changes occurring within administrative agencies generally involve both legislation and litigation, depending upon the individual agency.

Determining the law applicable to a specific situation can thus be very complicated. Each state has its own statutes passed by its legislature and its own cases decided by its courts, perhaps applicable in different parts of the state. The federal government also has laws, which may or may not be controlling, and cases decided by trial and appellate courts, as well as by the United States Supreme Court. There are also constitutions, both the federal constitution and individual state constitutions, which set out general principles that the courts interpret. A court may interpret a constitution to invalidate a statute, so that even though a statute has been passed as law, it may be unconstitutional and thus void. All of these complexities mean not only that the law can be difficult to determine but also that there are various ways in which it can change.

Legal change is a continuing process. The following chapters discuss this process, make generalizations, and provide examples from cases and statutes. Rather than provide specific legal guidance, the discussions are intended to provide an overview of legal issues that affect lesbians, gay men, bisexuals, and transgendered persons because of our sexuality. These issues include the regulation of our sexuality and discrimination against us, our education and our families, crimes against us and perpetrated by us, the intersection between health and the law, and finally our role in the legal profession. All of these issues continue to be shaped by the many lesbians, gay men, bisexuals, and transgendered persons who participate in legal processes.

Cases cited in
GAY MEN, LESBIANS,
AND THE LAW

Alison D. v. Virginia M., 77 N.Y.2d 651, 572 N.E.2d 27, 569 N.Y.S.2d 586 (1991).

Bowers v. Hardwick, 478 U.S. 186 (1986).

Bradwell v. Illinois, 83 U.S. (16 Wall.) 1872.

In re Breisch, 434 A.2d 815 (Pa. Super. Ct. 1981).

Commonwealth v. Carr, 398 Pa. Super. 306, 580 2d 1362 (1990).

Commonwealth v. Wasson, 842 S.W.2d 487 (Ky. 1992).

Chalk v. United States District Court, 840 F.2d 701 (9th Cir. 1988).

Curran v. Mount Diablo Boy Scouts, 23 Cal.App.4th 1307, 29 Cal.Rptr.2d 580 (1994).

Evans v. Romer, 854 P.2d 1270 (Colo. 1993).

Fricke v. Lynch, 491 F. Supp. 381 (D. R.I. 1980).

Gay and Lesbian Students Association v. Gohn, 850 F.2d 361 (8th Cir. 1988).

Gay Rights Coalition of Georgetown University Law Center v. Georgetown University, 536 A.2d 1 (D.C. App. 1987).

Hartogs v. Employers Mutual Liability, 89 Misc.2d 486 (N.Y. 1977).

In re Kimball, 33 N.Y. 2d 586, 347 N.Y.S.2d 453 (1973).

In re Kowalski, 478 N.W.2d 790 (Minn. App. 1991).

Lloyd v. Grella, 83 N.Y.2d 537, 611 N.Y.S.2d 799, 634 N.E.2d 171 (1994).

Loving v. Virginia, 388 U.S. 1 (1967).

Meyer v. Nebraska, 262 U.S. 390 (1923).

Miller v. Spicer, 822 F. Supp. 158 (D. Del. 1993).

Morrison v. State Board of Education, 461 P.2d 375 (Cal. 1969).

Pierce v. Society of Sisters, 268 U.S. 510 (1925).

Rowland v. Mad River Local School District, 470 U.S. 1009 (Brennan, J., dissenting).

Rose v. Locke, 423 U.S. 48 (1975).

School Board of Nassau County v. Arline, 480 U.S. 273 (1987).

Sinn v. Daily Nebraskan, 638 F. Supp. 143 (D. Neb. 1986).

Solmitz v. Maine School Administrative District No. 59, 495 A.2d 812 (Me. 1985).

Watkins v. United States Army, 875 F.2d 699 (9th Cir. 1989) (en banc).

White v. Thompson, 569 So. 2d 1181 (Miss. 1990).

Yost v. Board of Regents, not reported in F. Supp., 1993 WL 524757 (D. Md. 1993).

1

The Legal Regulation of Sexual Expression

Demonstrators disguised as Supreme Court justices Sandra Day O'Connor and Byron White seek to separate a kissing lesbian couple on the steps of the Supreme Court Building as part of a demonstration staged by activists to protest the Court's decision to uphold the conviction of a Georgia man under that state's sodomy laws.

GOVERNMENTAL REGULATION OF SEXUALITY is accomplished through the use of laws that criminalize certain sexual expressions. Although these laws are often known as "sodomy laws," the term "sex statutes" is now more accurate because of changes in how the laws have been written and interpreted in the recent past. These sex statutes are the legal force that criminalizes sexual expression between consenting adults, including lesbians and gay men.

The sex statutes can make each of us a criminal whether or not we are ever charged with a crime. Courts often use the existence of sex statutes in noncriminal matters. For example, in discrimination cases involving lesbians and gay men, courts often refer to the sex statutes as support for the conclusion that we should not be protected from discrimination. Likewise, in custody cases involving lesbian or gay parents, courts often cite the sex statutes as part of the reasoning for depriving the lesbian or gay parent of custody. Discrimination and custody are discussed more specifically in subsequent chapters, but such links with the criminalization of our sexual expression are important. By making us criminals, the sex statutes allow the courts and society to view us as undeserving to be protected from discrimination or to be parents.

The criminal sex statutes can also affect us in immediate and direct ways. Historically, a conviction under a sex statute could mean a sentence of death. Today, the punishment can range from a misdemeanor conviction resulting in a fine to a felony conviction with the possibility of life imprisonment. Despite this liberalization of punishment, the present sex statutes have historical roots.

Contemporary sex statutes are generally traced through Anglo-European history to early Christian religious law. In this tradition, sexuality that was not directly related to producing legitimate children was punishable as a "crime against nature" or a "crime against God." This meant that any sexual expression outside of marriage was a crime, regardless of whether the participants were of the same or different genders. It also meant that any sexual expression by married partners that was not directly related to the conception of a child—nonprocreative sex—was a crime. The existence and enforcement of these harsh laws varied through the centuries and in different geographical areas. Punishments also varied from public censure to burning at the stake. Although some recent historical scholarship has argued that many cultures tolerated a variety of sexual expression, the traditional view is that religious and later secular governments prohibited all nonprocreative sex and all sex outside of a married relationship.

As the traditional wide range of prohibitions gradually became more refined, lesbian and gay sexual expressions became a distinct subset of sexual crimes. Perhaps because officials feared that being specific about the actions that constituted homosexuality would encourage people to engage in these acts, most of the earlier laws against gay and lesbian sexuality are vague. Examples of early descriptions include "those who gave themselves up to works of lewdness with their own sex," the "unnatural lust of men with men or women with women," the "impurity of a woman with a woman," and a "man lying with another." The imprecision of "lewdness," "unnatural lust," and "impurity" contrast with the law's precision concerning punishments: death by burning at the stake, death followed by being burned at the stake, death by drowning, death by hanging, death by beheading, loss of all property, flogging in public, and banishment outside of the city.

Early American lawmakers adopted the preference for imprecision in the description of such crimes. Colonial legislators used catchall phrases such as "sodomy," "unnatural copulation," "buggery," and "crime against nature." These phrases became codified into the laws of the states. As late as 1968, every state had a statute that punished gay or lesbian sexual expression.

Today, almost half the states still have sex statutes in their criminal codes. These vary from state to state. Generally, these statutes use three distinct strategies to criminalize lesbian and gay sexual expression: the natural strategy, the anatomically specific strategy, and the gender-specific strategy. A state legislature is not limited to one strategy, and sometimes laws combine the strategies.

The natural strategy relies on the traditional wording of earlier laws prohibiting sexual expression. The laws are arcane in their language and vague in their intent. Examples of statutes using the natural strategy to criminalize gay and lesbian sex are those that punish "the crime against nature" in North Carolina and Louisiana, "the abominable and detestable crime against nature" in Michigan and Rhode Island, "the detestable and abominable crime against nature" in Mississippi and Oklahoma, and "the infamous crime against nature" in Arizona and Idaho. Other statutes also rely on "natural" understandings of other terms, although such statutes may not use the term "nature." For example, Florida's statute criminalizing "unnatural and lascivious" conduct, the United States Code of Military Justice section criminalizing "unnatural carnal copulation," and South Carolina's statute

Gay and lesbian activists demonstrate outside the Federal Courthouse in New York City's Foley Square on July 4, 1986. Those who support gay and lesbian civil rights are generally in agreement with a legal philosophy that argues that the government has little or no right to regulate sexual conduct that occurs in private between consenting adults.

criminalizing "the abominable crime of buggery" all employ the natural strategy of criminalizing lesbian and gay sexual expression.

Courts applying these statutes to specific cases have failed to arrive at common definitions. Courts have varied along a "narrow" to "broad" continuum of definitional interpretation. Under the narrow interpretations, courts restrict the criminalized activity to anal or oral sex between men. Some state courts have held that certain lesbian sexual expressions are "regrettably" not criminalized, usually prompting the legislature to quickly amend the statute. Generally, when state courts have applied this narrow view, legislatures have rewritten the statutes or passed additional sex statutes to cover a larger number of sexual acts.

Under the broad interpretations, courts have tended to include all nonprocreative sex and apply these statutes to both heterosexual and gay or lesbian sexual encounters. For example, the Nevada Supreme Court decided that its statute should "cover the entire field of unnatural acts of carnal copulation." Some courts have broadened the application of "crime against nature" at the first opportunity by declaring that the statute covers "all acts of unnatural carnal copulation in whatsoever form those acts may be perpetrated." Other courts have taken a more modest approach to expansion, rendering decisions limited to the specific sex acts before the court in the particular case. Sexual activities routinely found to be criminalized by broader interpretations include anal sex, fellatio, cunnilingus, and mutual masturbation.

Whether courts decide to interpret the natural strategy as applying narrowly or broadly, the obvious problem with this type of sex statute is its imprecision. Such imprecision can raise a constitutional question. Generally, under the due process clauses of the United States Constitution, a law must be understandable by an average person of ordinary intelligence. If a criminal statute does not clearly inform a person what is being prohibited, the law can be voided for vagueness. The courts of several states have held natural strategy statutes unconstitutional on the grounds that such language fails to inform the average person of common intelligence as to what is prohibited. The courts of other states have held natural strategy statutes constitutional. These courts reason that although the statute's language is vague, the way individual cases and individual judges apply the terms makes them constitutional. Still other state courts have held the phrase "crime against nature" to be inherently understandable.

Although the state laws vary, such different conclusions about constitutionality cannot be explained by the variance in the statutes alone. Because each state court system has the independence to interpret its own statutes, the high court in one state may find a sex statute unconstitutional but a neighboring state's high court could conclude the opposite. If state courts rely upon their own state constitutions (which usually contain terms such as due process, similar to the federal constitution), each state's decision will be independent. This independence will prevail unless the state court's decision violates a federal constitutional right.

A decision from the United States Supreme Court holding that natural strategies were unconstitutionally vague under the federal constitution would void such statutes in every state. There would be no more inconsistent opinions between states and no more uncertainty if state courts had not yet ruled on their particular statutes. However, the United States Supreme Court has held the natural strategy constitutional. In *Rose v. Locke*, decided in 1975, the Court upheld a Tennessee "crime against nature" statute as constitutional under the federal constitution. The Court found that the statute met the requirements of constitutional due process because all that is required is that "the law give sufficient warning that men [sic] may conduct themselves as to avoid that which is forbidden." The Court stated that "viewed against this standard, the phrase 'crime against nature' is no more vague than many other terms used to describe criminal offenses at common law." Thus, unless *Rose v. Locke* is overturned by the United States Supreme Court (an unlikely prospect), only state courts will declare their state's sex statute unconstitutional.

When a state court declares a sex statute unconstitutionally vague, the state legislature has two options. It can do nothing, thus effectively removing that sex statute from the enforceable laws of the state, although the law may still be "on the books." Or it can attempt to redraft the law to comply with constitutional requirements. Such redrafting has resulted in the second strategy used in sex statutes, the anatomically specific strategy.

Sex statutes using the anatomically specific strategy describe what body parts have to be involved before a sexual act is punishable. Unless the statute contains other limits, it applies to all sex acts that include the listed body parts. The anatomically specific statutes generally focus on sexual acts involving the sexual organs (genitals) of one person and the mouth or anus of another. Thus, sex statutes using an anatomically specific strategy can criminalize gay, lesbian, or heterosexual sexual encounters.

The statutes vary from state to state in the types of sexual activity they criminalize. Nevertheless, Alabama, Georgia, Utah, Virginia, Minnesota, Washington, D.C., Texas, and Kansas each specifically prohibit oral–genital and genital–anal contact. However, as in all criminal law, interpreting the statutes and deciding what activities they apply to is left to the courts. Courts have generally refused to include the touching, stroking, or penetration of the vagina or anus by anything other than a sex organ. Such common sexual activity as mutual masturbation, tribadism, touching or stroking of genitals by hands, kissing, and petting would not necessarily be criminalized, especially if the statute mentioned only oral–genital or anal–genital contact. In addition, at least one court suggested that the contact must be between flesh and flesh, so that contact between flesh and clothing does not fall within the statutory language.

The third strategy used in sex statutes consists of adding gender specificity. The addition of a same-sex requirement to one of the above types of sex statutes is meant to directly target the sexual activities of lesbians and gay men. The same-gender requirement criminalizes sexual expressions between men or between women but excludes those same expressions if they occur between a man and a woman. For example, Montana's sex statute criminalizes "sexual contact or sexual intercourse between two persons of the same sex." The statute defines sexual contact as "any touching of the sexual or other intimate parts of the person of another for the purposes of arousing or gratifying the sexual desire of either party." Tennessee forbids anyone to "engage in consensual sexual penetration" with a person of the same gender. Sexual penetration is defined as "sexual intercourse, cunnilingus, fellatio, anal intercourse, or any other intrusion, however slight, of any part of a person's body or of any object into the genital or anal openings of the victim's, the defendant's or any other person's body."

While the numbers of gay men and lesbians who are actively pursued by the police for violating the sex statutes is relatively small, there are adult gay men and lesbians who have been arrested or convicted. Many lesbians and gay men have entered guilty or no contest pleas when charged under these statutes, often because of the fear of publicity. However, some lesbians and gay men have challenged these sex statutes with legal arguments. These arguments often depend upon the type of strategy the particular sex statute uses. For example, someone charged with a natural strategy statute could argue that the statute was too vague. Likewise, someone charged with an anatomically specific statute could argue that the particular act was not criminalized.

Further, the usual criminal law defenses would apply, depending upon the particular circumstances of the case. The most important of these is the requirement of corroborating evidence. Because the sex statutes prohibit participation in a particular act, regardless of whether

Religious fundamentalists express their opinion of gay and lesbian civil rights during the National Gay and Lesbian March on Washington in April 1993. Scriptural admonitions and religious dogma are often cited as justifications for homophobia.

or not each person consents, both parties involved can be charged with the crime. This also means that each person is an accomplice to the other person's criminal act. Generally, a conviction cannot be obtained purely on the testimony of an accomplice. There must be other evidence, known as corroborating evidence, besides the word of the person who was also engaged in the act. This could be physical evidence or another person hearing language or noise that indicated sexual activity.

The requirement of corroboration is one reason that criminal prosecutions against consenting adult lesbians and gay men are relatively rare: they can be difficult to prove. The large majority of prosecutions under the sex statutes do not concern consensual acts, and many concern heterosexual encounters. For example, in *Rose v. Locke,* the man who challenged the vagueness of the Tennessee natural strategy sex statute had been convicted of using a butcher knife to force a female neighbor into a sexual encounter. The prosecution of such an act would be more appropriate under rape or forced sex statutes. However, prosecutions often include a violation of a sex statute because it may be easier to prove. Because of the use of the sex statutes to prosecute violent acts, some lesbians and gay men believe that the sex statutes are harmless. Most lesbian and gay legal advocates disagree. As long as gay and lesbian sexuality is criminalized, gays and lesbians remain in danger of arrest, prosecution, and conviction for sexual expressions. By criminalizing gay and lesbian sexuality, the sex statutes also function to legitimize other forms of discrimination.

For these reasons, lesbian and gay legal advocates have long fought for the abolition of these laws. Their most ambitious effort consisted of a constitutional attack that would have affected all statutes criminalizing consensual sex. The basis for such an attack was the constitutional theory of privacy. In order to mount such an attack, however, there had to be a person willing and able to come forward. Although there were many lesbians and gay men who were willing, the courts rejected their ability to challenge the statutes. These rejections were based upon the procedural requirement of standing. Standing requires that the person challenging the constitutionality of the law have a "sufficient stake in the

25

Many traditional sodomy statutes, such as the Georgia law that these protestors came to the steps of the state capitol to demonstrate against in 1990, rely on a definition of certain sexual acts as inherently "unnatural" or "perverted."

outcome." While it certainly seems that gay men and lesbians have a stake in the sex statutes criminalizing their sexual expression, the courts held that there must be a real threat of prosecution. Thus, for many years courts rebuffed the challenges of lesbians and gay men to the very statutes that made them criminals. The fact that actual prosecutions of gay men and lesbians were rare insulated the sex statutes from challenges, even though they were routinely used for other purposes.

In 1982, gay and lesbian activists located the nearly perfect case with which to argue that a sex statute violated the right to privacy. The facts leading up to the arrest of Michael Hardwick, a 28-year-old white gay man, demonstrate the manner in which gay men and lesbians are routinely harassed and the role of the sex statutes in that harassment. Hardwick worked in a gay bar in Atlanta. One morning after work, Hardwick left the bar with a beer in his hand. He decided he did not want the beer and threw it in a trash can outside the bar. A police officer, Torrick, stopped Hardwick and asked him several questions, including where he had thrown the beer bottle and what he was doing on the street at 7:00 A.M. Hardwick's answer that he worked at the bar identified him as gay because the bar was a well-known gay meeting place. For 20 minutes, Hardwick sat in the back of the police car while the officer drove. Officer Torrick finally issued a ticket for drinking in public.

The ticket required Hardwick to appear in court, but it had a discrepancy about whether the court date was on a Tuesday or a Wednesday. Apparently, it was on Tuesday, because two hours after the court time on Tuesday, Torrick came to Hardwick's home with an arrest warrant. Hardwick was not home, however. When his roommate told him later that a police officer had been there, Hardwick went to the county clerk. He told the clerk that a police officer had already been to his house with an arrest warrant. The clerk said that was impossible, because it usually takes at least 48 hours to process a warrant. Apparently, Torrick had personally processed the warrant, the first time he had done this in 10 years. Hardwick paid a $50 fine for drinking in public and thought everything was settled.

About three weeks later, Torrick returned to Hardwick's house with the arrest warrant. The front door to the house was open. Torrick entered the house, stood by Hardwick's bedroom door, and watched him having oral sex with another man. Torrick then entered the bedroom and arrested Hardwick and his companion for violating Georgia's sex statute.

Hardwick was charged and "bound over to the Superior Court." Although the district attorney decided not to prosecute the case "unless further evidence developed," the arrest and court appearance were sufficient to confer standing on Hardwick, establishing his legal ability to challenge the statute. Hardwick became a plaintiff in a civil rights suit challenging the Georgia statute in federal court on constitutional grounds. A married heterosexual couple joined Hardwick's action against the statute, which makes no reference to gender or marriage. However, the court dismissed the married couple's claims, concluding that they lacked evidence showing a likelihood of prosecution.

Hardwick lost his claim in federal court, but won when he appealed to the United States District Court for the Eleventh Circuit. Judge Frank Johnson, a well-known civil rights champion from Montgomery, Alabama, wrote an opinion in which he found that the Georgia statute implicated the "fundamental right" to an activity that is "quintessentially private." The state of Georgia sought review by the United States Supreme Court. The Supreme Court—the ultimate arbiter of federal constitutional doctrine—agreed to review the case, a relatively rare occurrence given the number of requests for review filed with the Court. Although there were leaks that the Court was ready to rule in favor of Hardwick (after retiring, one justice said that he had made a mistake by not ruling in favor of Hardwick), the Supreme Court ruled against Hardwick by a vote of five to four. In *Bowers v. Hardwick,* decided in 1986, the Court ruled that any claim that "homosexual sodomy" is protected by the right to privacy is "facetious, at best." In other words, gay men and lesbians have no federal constitutional right to sexual expression.

The Court's opinion in *Hardwick* has met overwhelming disapproval. Many legal scholars outside the lesbian and gay legal community have written scathing critiques of it. Most agree with the dissenting justices, who concluded that the right to privacy should include all consensual private sexual encounters. Many scholars criticized the Court's majority opinion for interpreting the issue as being whether "homosexual sodomy" rather than privacy for all persons is a fundamental right. Further, they described Justice Byron White's concurring opinion that concluded that sodomy has always and everywhere been subject to criminal sanction as a homophobic misuse of history.

The *Hardwick* decision was a defeat for lesbian and gay legal advocates. A decision in favor of Hardwick by the United States Supreme Court would have meant that states could not criminalize lesbian or gay sexual expression. Nevertheless, the decision has provoked renewed organizing by lesbian, gay, and bisexual activists, as well as many sympathetic heterosexuals, in support of lesbian and gay rights and freedom of sexual expression. Further, many lesbian and gay legal advocates have continued to attack the sex statutes.

For example, Michigan and Texas courts have found their state sex statutes unconstitutional under their respective state constitutions. Because these cases were decided based upon the state constitutions, the statutes were invalidated. The United States Supreme Court's decision is not applicable because *Hardwick* involved the federal constitution.

A crowd estimated at 200,000 attended the March on Washington for Lesbian and Gay Rights in 1987. Opponents of lesbian and gay civil rights sometimes argue that homosexuals do not constitute a true minority in that their classification as such is based on behavior rather than on some essentially immutable characteristic, like race or gender. One counter to such an argument is that religious faith is likewise an element of behavior rather than inborn identity and yet is guarded by constitutional protections.

One of the most important state cases after *Hardwick* is *Commonwealth v. Wasson.* In 1992, the Supreme Court of Kentucky found the Kentucky sex statutes unconstitutional under the state constitution. Those statutes combined the natural, anatomically specific, and gender specific strategies to criminalize lesbian and gay sexual expression. They prohibited "deviate sexual intercourse with another of the same sex," which was defined as including "any act of sexual gratification involving the sex organs of one person and the mouth or anus of another." Jeffrey Wasson was not arrested for violating the Kentucky sex statutes, but for "soliciting" another person to violate the statutes. The incident involved a 20- to 25-minute conversation during which he invited another man to "come home" with him. When the man prodded Wasson for details, Wasson suggested sexual acts that would have violated the Kentucky sex statutes. Wasson's conversational partner was a police officer participating in an undercover operation. He arrested Wasson on the basis of the conversation, which he had taped.

Wasson moved to have the charges against him dismissed on the grounds that the sex statutes violated the state constitution. The trial judge agreed, but the state appealed. The appellate court also agreed with Wasson's arguments, so the state appealed again. The Supreme Court of Kentucky agreed with the lower courts and with Wasson, stating that "the guarantees of individual liberty provided in our 1891 Kentucky Constitution offer greater protection of the right of privacy than provided by the Federal Constitution."

The Kentucky Supreme Court's decision is important because it demonstrates a state's ability to reach a different conclusion from *Hardwick*. The Kentucky court carved out an exception to *Hardwick* by delineating the importance that individual autonomy and privacy was given by the founders of the state of Kentucky and in the writing of the Kentucky Constitution and Bill of Rights. In addition, the Kentucky Supreme Court specifically repudiated the United States Supreme Court's reasoning in *Hardwick* as misdirected.

The Kentucky Supreme Court's decision should encourage challenges to other sex statutes under specific state constitutions because the Kentucky Constitution is similar to that of many other states. It does not have any unique language that mandates this particular result. A few state constitutions do include a specific right to privacy, which would give added weight to a privacy challenge to a sex statute.

Privacy challenges require sexual expression that occurs in private. Sexual expressions that occur in public are criminalized in every state, but the definition of public can be very loose. The inside of a parked car, under a beach pier, and in front of a picture window facing the street have all been held by courts to be public places. Further, the definition of private generally includes an implicit limit of two persons. The introduction of a third person, either as witness or participant, generally renders the sexual encounter legally public.

Privacy challenges also require sexual expression that is consensual. Obviously, Locke wielding a butcher knife against his neighbor is not something that should be protected by privacy principles. However, the notion of consent also includes the implicit limit of adulthood, based upon the legal belief that minors do not have the capacity to consent. Just as minors cannot enter into a contract to buy a piece of land, they cannot legally consent to a sexual encounter. But while it is not a criminal act to sell a minor a piece of land, it is a crime to engage in sexual activity with a minor. This may be true even if one is a minor oneself.

All states have statutes criminalizing sex with a minor. These statutes differ according to the ages at which one is considered a minor, which sometimes vary for females and males. To further complicate matters, most states have a statutory "scheme"—rather than a single statute—that covers sexual encounters with minors. Such schemes contain graduated degrees of criminal responsibility that fluctuate with the age of the minor. For example, sex with a minor who is under 12 might be a first-degree offense; sex with a minor who is under 14 might be a second-degree offense; and sex with a minor who is under 16 might be a third-degree offense. Such a scheme may also fluctuate with the age of the defendant. For example, a defendant may have to be at least 18 or 21 in order to be charged with a criminal act. Generally, these schemes do not impose different age requirements depending upon whether the sexual encounter is heterosexual or lesbian/gay. This is true even though the actual prohibitions may be in different statutes: "rape" statutes for heterosexual encounters and "deviate" or "sodomy" statutes for lesbian and gay encounters. While lesbian and gay legal advocates in Great Britain have struggled many years against laws that establish 18 as the legal age of consent for heterosexual encounters and 21 for homosexual encounters, advocates in the United States have not faced a similar situation. Instead, they have struggled against laws criminalizing their sexual expression, even that occurring between consenting adults in private. The sex statutes are just one form of the pervasive discrimination that continues against gays and lesbians.

2

Discrimination Against Sexual Minorities

WHERE ONE IS ABLE to live, work, and travel can be limited by other people. A property owner may choose not to rent or sell a home to someone, an employer may choose not to hire a particular applicant, or a hotel manager may say that there are no rooms available. Most of the time the law is not concerned with such choices, preferring not to interfere with the freedom of the property owner, employer, or hotel manager. There are times, however, when the exercise of such freedom is termed discrimination. At such times, the choice to deny another person something is said to be based upon prejudice and bias. In a legal sense, prejudice and bias occur when someone is being judged on the basis of a group identity, such as being lesbian or gay, rather than on their individual circumstances. The law has been used to challenge discrimination on the basis of religion, race, and ethnicity, and more recently, gender and physical ability as well as sexual orientation.

The extent to which the law should prohibit the exercise of prejudice is a long-standing legal debate. Important to this debate is the distinction between the public and private realms. The public realm, exemplified by the government itself, is generally held to a higher standard of nondiscrimination. This standard is rooted in the notion of democracy: the government is supposed to represent and benefit everyone. On the other hand, the private realm, exemplified by a person on the street, is generally held to a lesser standard of nondiscrimination. This standard is rooted in the notion of individual freedom: an individual should be free to think and act as she or he believes appropriate. Yet as the experience of most minorities suggests, discrimination by private individuals, who often control access to housing, employment, education, or public accommodations such as hotels and restaurants, can have more of an impact on daily life than discrimination by the government.

As originally drafted, the Constitution of the United States was more concerned with the distribution of power between levels of government—the states and the newly formed federal government—than with relations between private citizens, or even between citizens and the government. The addition of the first 10 amendments, known as the Bill of Rights, sought to limit the federal government's power to control individual citizens (meaning of course only white men over 21 years of age). Not until after the Civil War did additional amendments restrict the power of state governments to control citizens, a category now expanded to mean all males, including those of African descent who had formerly been slaves. These amendments, often known as the Reconstruction Amendments, include the 14th Amendment's famous proclamation that states shall not deny to any person "equal protection of the laws." Although this protection has been extended to include the federal government, courts interpreting the 14th Amendment have limited it to governmental actors. Under this "state action" doctrine, private discrimination and social injustices do not fall under the 14th Amendment.

Nevertheless, the notion of equal protection—equality—remains important as the constitutional basis for arguments that the government may not discriminate because of group identity, including sexual orientation. Courts applying the equal protection clause of the Constitution have held that there is a hierarchy of identities that merit protection. Racial, ethnic, and religious identities occupy the highest

In echoing Bill Clinton's famous campaign strategy for his successful run for the presidency in 1992, the placards carried by these participants in a January 1993 protest in New York City explain why the issues of gay men and lesbians in the military, in particular, and gay and lesbian civil rights in general are such important ones.

tier within this hierarchy; such groups are known as suspect classes. The general hallmarks of a suspect class include requirements that it is a social minority that has been historically discriminated against and continues to be relatively politically powerless. Further, the members of the group must possess "immutable" characteristics that are identifiable.

Laws that make distinctions based upon such categories are subject to strict scrutiny and are generally not upheld. For example, a law providing that persons of African descent could not attend college would be subject to strict scrutiny and declared unconstitutional. Gender identity occupies a middle tier; it is often called a "quasi-suspect class." Laws that make gender classifications are subject to a less strict scrutiny and are upheld if the government can convince a court that there is an important reason for making such a classification. The lowest of the three tiers of equal protection analysis is occupied by groups that are not deemed suspect or quasi-suspect classes, such as lesbians and gay men. As long as governmental discrimination against lesbians and gay men is analyzed under this lowest tier, the law will be upheld if the government can convince a court that the law is rationally related to a legitimate purpose.

Discrimination by the military and quasi-military agencies such as the Federal Bureau of Investigation (FBI) and Central Intelligence Agency (CIA) has been the subject of many challenges by lesbians and gay men under the equal protection doctrine. There is no question that federal policies declaring lesbians and gay men "unfit," "undesirable security risks," or "incompatible" with federal government employment involve governmental action, and thus the Constitution is clearly applicable. These governmental regulations explicitly authorize discrimination against homosexuality, so it is quite clear that the judgment is based upon a group rather than individual identity. What is contested, however, is whether or not discrimination against lesbians and gay men is unconstitutional.

Legal advocates have argued that courts should consider lesbians and gay men a suspect class and thus analyze discrimination claims under a higher tier of scrutiny. In applying the hallmarks of a suspect class, courts have found that lesbians and gay men are a statistical minority that has been historically discriminated against. Courts have surprisingly been less willing to conclude that lesbians and gay men are politically powerless today. The requirement that the group be relatively powerless derives from a concern that courts not grant constitutional protection to groups that could gain such protections through other political means, such as voting or lobbying. A few courts have relied upon contemporary journalistic accounts of lesbian and gay pride parades or political organizing to conclude that lesbians and gay men could easily influence elected officials and therefore do not need judicial protection.

The classic hallmark of suspect-class identification that has caused the most problem, however, is the requirement of immutable and identifiable characteristics. Courts interpret immutable to mean a characteristic that cannot be mutated or changed; one that is constant throughout life; one that is given at birth. Discussions of the applicability of this factor lead to debates about whether sexual orientation is a biological given that does not change (like eye color) or whether it can change throughout one's life (like one's choice of friends or lovers). Discussions also involve beliefs about whether or not sexual orientation is identifiable or perceptible by a casual observer. There are probably as many different opinions as the number of people who have thought about these questions. Yet in applying the suspect-class standard, courts have tended to isolate the factors of immutability and perceptibility, generally concluding that there is no proof that lesbian and gay identity is unchanging and observable. Courts have thus denied lesbians and gay men suspect-class status. This is true even though religious identity has been given suspect-class status, despite its likewise not always being unchanging or perceptible.

Legal advocates for the rights of lesbians and gay men have not admitted defeat when courts have decided that lesbians and gay men do not constitute a suspect class. Instead, they have noted that even if the lowest tier of scrutiny is applied, the equal protection doctrine requires that the discrimination be rationally related to a legitimate governmental purpose. Usually, almost any reason that the government provides can meet this standard. However, courts have increasingly required the government to prove that the discrimination really does have a rational

A former air force captain salutes at the grave of Technical Sergeant Leonard Matlovich, who became a symbol of the gay rights movement after being discharged from the air force in 1978 once his sexual orientation was disclosed. "When I was in the military, they gave me a medal for killing two men—and a discharge for loving one," Matlovich once explained.

basis. For example, courts considering equal protection challenges to the exclusion of gay men and lesbians from military employment have begun to decide that prejudice is not rational. Thus, the military cannot rely upon its previous justifications for excluding lesbians and gay men, such as preserving discipline and morale. Courts are beginning to conclude that the threats to discipline and morale are not from lesbians and gay men, but from those heterosexual members of the military who may be prejudiced against lesbians and gay men. While maintaining discipline and morale are legitimate interests of the government, these interests cannot rationally be achieved by catering to private prejudices.

Discrimination in the military has also prompted other types of constitutional challenges. In addition to equal protection arguments, lesbians and gay men discharged from the military for revealing their sexual orientation have relied upon the First Amendment's guarantee that the government will not infringe free speech. There have been many who have been discharged because they said they were lesbian or gay, sometimes in public speeches or newspaper interviews. Others have been discharged because they revealed their sexual orientation in what is known as a "symbolic speech act," such as marching in a lesbian and gay pride parade. Still others have revealed their sexual orientation when directly asked by one of their military superiors. In all of these cases, lesbians and gay men have argued that the government is infringing upon their speech because they are being discharged for something they have said. The government has argued that the discharge from the military is not based upon what they said (that they were lesbian or gay) but is based upon the meaning of what they said (if one is lesbian or gay one will commit homosexual acts). Courts have generally accepted this distinction, but the military has changed the wording of many of the regulations that govern discharge of lesbians and gay men. The newest regulations do not permit members of the military to directly ask other members about their sexual orientation.

Constitutional challenges to the military's exclusion of lesbians and gay men often force courts to confront situations of individual injustice. One of the most interesting cases is that of Perry Watkins. When Watkins received a draft notice during the Vietnam War, he returned it with a check by the "yes" box for "homosexual tendencies" because he knew he was gay. The army sent him to a psychiatrist who engaged in explicit conversations with Watkins concerning his preferences and practices of gay male sex. Nevertheless, the psychiatrist certified Watkins as not gay. Watkins recalls that every gay white person he knew who checked the "yes" box for "homosexual tendencies" was not inducted, but as a black gay person he was inducted. During his time in the army, Watkins requested numerous discharges because of his gayness but was always denied. Ultimately, he made a career of the military, a career that included official duties such as entertaining while dressed in drag. After 15 years of service, the military denied him—upon the basis of his sexuality—a routine reenlistment. Watkins sued the army. The court avoided the constitutional issues and decided the case based upon an estoppel theory, meaning that because the army knew that he was gay from the very beginning of his career, it was estopped—in the interests of fairness—from taking negative action on that basis at this late date, five years short of a retirement that would provide him with a substantial pension.

Discrimination in the military is an important contemporary legal issue. The military and government are the largest employers in the United States. Further, the military often reflects the biases of society. In the case of homosexuality, this bias is bluntly expressed in written form. Thus, having it declared unconstitutional would have an important symbolic effect.

Other sometimes less explicit biases in the military also combine with the explicit bias against lesbians and gay men. For example, women are proportionately more likely to be discharged for violating regulations prohibiting homosexuality than are men; estimates range from 3–4 times more likely to 10 times more likely. Some explain this disparity in terms of the prevalent sexism of the military and the use of lesbian baiting to control all women, even if they are not lesbians. Further, persons of color are disproportionately represented in the military, with numbers ranging from 27 percent to 51 percent depending upon the branch. The case of Perry Watkins demonstrates that the military may overlook sexual orientation when drafting men of color, while declining to draft white men who raise the issue of sexual orientation. There is also some evidence that gay men and lesbians of color are more likely to be discharged from the military than their white counterparts. It is important to remember, too, that discharge from employment is not the only penalty imposed by the military. The military may also court-martial lesbians and gay men because of their sexual orientation and has sentenced many to serve time in military prisons. There is some evidence that racial, ethnic, and class biases may influence the military's choice as to whether to discharge or court-martial.

In addition to challenging discrimination as unconstitutional, groups discriminated against can also agitate for new laws to prohibit such discrimination. Such laws can often regulate private as well as governmental acts. Interestingly, the federal government's authority to pass such laws derives from its power to regulate interstate commerce. Thus, federal laws regulating private employers often contain a requirement, such as a minimum number of employees, that relates to a presumed impact upon interstate commerce.

The most comprehensive federal law prohibiting discrimination is the 1964 Civil Rights Act, which prohibits discrimination in employment, housing, education, and public accommodations such as hotels and restaurants. This legislation grew out of the civil rights movement, which was primarily concerned with racial justice for African Americans. In addition to race and religion, however, the act includes "sex" in its protected identities. The inclusion of sex is not attributable to feminists or advocates of gender justice, but to a conservative senator who believed that the addition of sex would guarantee that the bill would not pass. It did pass and became law, however, and serves as an important tool against discrimination, including gender discrimination.

But the act does not mention sexual orientation. Many lesbians and gay men have therefore argued that sexual orientation should be protected under the category of "sex." The argument that discrimination on the basis of sexual orientation is really discrimination on the basis of sex does have some appeal. If, for example, a person who has a sexual attraction for women is a man, this (male) person would be heterosexual and not subject to discrimination, but if this person is a woman, she is a lesbian and is subject to discrimination. Such arguments, as well as the arguments on behalf of transsexuals who undergo gender reassignment surgeries, have been rejected by the courts. Courts have reasoned that if lesbians were being treated differently from gay men, it would be "sex" discrimination, but since discrimination on the basis of homosexuality includes both genders, it is not sex discrimination.

Because gay men and lesbians are excluded from federal civil rights legislation, their advocates have proposed that Congress pass a lesbian and gay civil rights act, either by amending the Civil Rights Act of

1964 to include sexual orientation or passing an entirely new law modeled on the 1964 act. To date, bills have been drafted, but none have been voted upon by Congress. Many people are hopeful that such legislation will be passed before the end of the century.

Meanwhile, lesbian and gay activists have focused on getting anti-discrimination laws passed at state and local levels. State and local laws have the benefit of being able to regulate more completely. Unlike federal laws, state or local laws need not be based upon interstate commerce, or upon any commerce at all. States, and by extension local

These members of the San Francisco chapter of the Queer Scouts were not especially impressed by a 1992 decision of the United Way that the local Boy Scouts of America chapters be given five years to reform their antigay and antilesbian policies. The Queer Scouts had been hoping for a more immediate remedy.

governments, possess general powers to regulate for the good of their citizens. This can be done through the state constitution, which can provide more protections (but not less) than the federal constitution. It can also be done through statutes passed by state legislatures. States also have regulations promulgated by state agencies, such as the department of insurance. States also rely upon unwritten law, known as common law, which is interpreted and applied by the courts.

Taking all these different kinds of law into consideration, every state has some laws prohibiting discrimination. At times, such laws have been narrowly interpreted so that sexual orientation is excluded from protection. At other times, courts have interpreted state laws more expansively. State courts have also relied upon common law principles. For example, a California court considered the case of a gay male Eagle Scout, Timothy Curran, who was denied the routinely granted status of scoutmaster by the Boy Scouts of America. Curran was a model Boy Scout who had achieved such honors as being selected to attend the National Jamboree. Curran enjoyed the recreational aspects of being a Boy Scout, such as camping, but he also valued the training in journalism he received in the Boy Scout program. It was through his journalistic endeavors that the Boy Scouts became aware of his sexuality. Curran wrote an article for the *Gay Youth Community News* describing his decision to bring a male date to his high school prom: "This was my last chance to say with actions as well as words, 'Gay is okay, gay people are as good as straight people and can do anything they can.'" When Curran became 18, he applied to be scoutmaster, but the Boy Scouts denied the request because his "unusual lifestyle" was "inconsistent with the basic principles of scouting."

Curran sued the Boy Scouts. A trial court concluded that this treatment of the gay Boy Scout violated a common law right of fairness. The court also ruled that the Boy Scout organization may have violated California's antidiscrimination act. The court reasoned that the law's particular references to classifications such as sex and race were meant to be illustrative and not restrictive. Thus, the court did not require "sexual orientation" to be specifically listed but interpreted the statute broadly as mandating equality. The Boy Scouts vigorously appealed the trial court's rulings, arguing that the application of state laws in favor of the gay Eagle Scout violated the organization's constitutional rights. The California appellate court agreed with the Boy Scouts, upholding their decision to deny scoutmaster status to Curran because he was gay. The Boy Scout case demonstrates that the Constitution is a double-edged sword that can be used to override state laws prohibiting discrimination.

Nevertheless, state laws are important in preventing discrimination. The more specific the state law, the more chance that courts will apply it rigorously. California has joined a number of states that specifically prohibit discrimination on the basis of sexual orientation. The states with statewide statutes include Wisconsin (the first, in 1982), Massachusetts, Hawaii, Connecticut, California, Minnesota, and New Jersey. Many states have witnessed intensive efforts to pass these statutes, but numerous failures often precede the successes. For example, in New York a draft bill has been ready for many years, but conservative legislators have blocked the bill from even being discussed or voted upon. Victories in a few states hold out the promise that defeats in other states are only temporary.

At the local level, governments can pass ordinances that concern a broad spectrum of issues, including discrimination by private persons. There are now more than 100 towns, cities, and counties that have laws prohibiting discrimination on the basis of sexual orientation. Sometimes, these ordinances only concern discrimination by the local government itself, for example, prohibiting the government from discriminating in employment or provision of services such as police and fire protection. While a few of these ordinances have been in effect since the mid-1970s, such as those in East Lansing, Michigan, and Berkeley, California, most are much more recent. Passing these ordinances has often provoked intense debates in local communities. In many instances, there have been referendums, recalls, repeals, and registration drives.

These local laws have also been the subject of statewide opposition. In several states, some citizens have agitated for a statewide law that would prohibit local communities from passing laws protecting lesbians and gay men from discrimination. Most often, these statewide efforts have taken the form of initiatives to amend the state constitution. The voters of Colorado, with 53 percent voting in favor, recently passed one such initiative. This constitutional amendment, known as Amendment 2, prohibits local governments and all branches of the state government from enacting, adopting, or enforcing any statute, regulation, or policy "whereby homosexual, lesbian, or bisexual orientation, conduct, practices, or relationships" shall give rise to a claim of minority or protected status or any claim of discrimination. This amendment repealed all existing city laws that protected lesbians, gay men, and bisexuals from discrimination, such as those in Aspen, Boulder, and Denver. This amendment also prohibits any future laws, either state or local, that might protect lesbians, gay men, and bisexuals from discrimination, either by public entities or private individuals.

Legal advocates of lesbians, gay men, and bisexuals reacted quickly to Amendment 2. They instituted a case arguing that the amendment was unconstitutional under the United States Constitution. As the federal constitution, the United States Constitution is the supreme law of the land. Even state constitutions cannot violate provisions of the federal constitution. Although such legal advocates had many arguments in their favor, one of their most important was that Amendment 2 violated the federal constitution's 14th Amendment, notably the equal protection clause. Just as in the military context, they argued, such discrimination targets a suspect class. Certainly, the passage of such an amendment disproves any contention that lesbians and gay men have great political power. Legal advocates also argued that even if the lowest standard of equal protection review is applied, such discrimination is not rational. Both of these arguments merited serious attention from the courts.

But their most successful argument was that Amendment 2 disadvantages gays, lesbians, and bisexuals by making it more difficult for this group—and only this group—to pass legislation. This disadvantage, based upon group status, violates the federal equal protection clause. It is a violation because access to political processes such as the ability to pass legislation is a fundamental right that must be distributed equally.

The highest court in Colorado thus found, in *Evans v. Romer,* that it is a denial of equal protection to "fence out" any group from political avenues, such as local ordinances, that are generally available to other groups. If the amendment said that no person could be protected from discrimination by local laws, this would not violate equal protection (although it might be unconstitutional on a different basis). But because the amendment provides that persons belonging to a specific group—lesbians, gay men, and bisexuals—cannot be protected by local laws, this violates equal protection.

The Colorado decision in *Evans v. Romer* is not the end of antigay initiatives. Colorado is only one of many states with such antigay initiatives before the voters, legislators, and courts. Anti-gay-and-lesbian organizations have targeted several states for initiatives limiting discrimination claims by lesbians, gay men, and bisexuals. The litigation surrounding such initiatives involves increasingly sophisticated legal theories on both sides.

While many advocates of lesbians, gay men, and bisexuals have devoted themselves to legal battles against anti-gay-and-lesbian initia-tives, to agitating for legislative protections on local, state, and federal levels, and to litigating claims on constitutional grounds, some theorists have questioned the long-term goal of preventing discrimination. Although lesbians and gay men certainly need protection from both governments and private persons with the power to give effect to their prejudices, there may be a way in which laws against discrimination on the basis of sexual orientation could backfire. Most laws prohibiting discrimination on the basis of sexual orientation define it as meaning "heterosexuality, homosexuality, or bisexuality." While including het-erosexuality does have a leveling effect, it also means that lesbians and gay men cannot "discriminate" against heterosexuals. Such discrimina-tion may seem farfetched at first. But imagine a national lesbian conference, intended for lesbians only. Imagine a civil suit brought by a heterosexual married couple on the basis of an antidiscrimination law that includes sexual orientation. This couple wants to go to the conference so that they can convince the lesbians in attendance that it is better to be heterosexual. Imagine a court order requiring the lesbian

The Colorado electorate's approval of the state's controversial Amendment 2 in the 1992 elections sparked protests across the nation by advocates of sexual tolerance. These two young women let their feelings be known at a rally in New York City's Central Park in January 1993. Amendment 2 prohibited the outlawing of discrimination based on sexual preference.

conference to allow Mr. and Mrs. X to attend, because to exclude them discriminates on the basis of heterosexuality. Imagine Mr. X speaking out at programs on safe sex or legal issues and telling lesbians they should listen to him because he is a man and knows better. Imagine Mrs. X handing out leaflets that proclaim the joy she has found in her heterosexual marriage and offer advice on how to dress more "like a lady."

Some might argue that a lesbian conference should not exclude anyone, regardless of their sexual orientation. One strand of this argument is that discrimination is always wrong, no matter who discriminates and who is discriminated against. Another strand of this argument is that those who have been discriminated against should know how bad discrimination is and for them to discriminate against others is hypocritical. Others believe, however, that there is a difference between discrimination by dominant groups (such as heterosexuals) and attempts by minority groups to gather together. This belief is based upon the power differences between majority and minority groups throughout history and in contemporary society.

Despite such varied beliefs, the law generally makes no distinction between majority and minority groups in terms of discrimination. It would be discrimination for lesbians, gays, and bisexuals to exclude heterosexuals based upon their identity as heterosexuals. Under the equal protection doctrine, so-called reverse discrimination is firmly established in American law. For example, constitutional issues arise when an organization reserves a position for a racial minority. Likewise, constitutional issues arise when an organization only admits women. Unless an organization can argue that the Constitution does not apply or that its own constitutional rights are at stake (like the Boy Scouts did), then such discrimination is unconstitutional.

The final issue to be considered under the broad term of discrimination is the extent to which lesbians, gay men, and bisexuals are included in "diversity." Diversity has generally replaced the notion of "affirmative action," but it is in turn being replaced by "multiculturalism." No matter which word is used, the idea is the same: that minorities should be included in all facets of life, including where one lives, works, and plays. This idea goes a step further than nondiscrimination because it proposes that not only should group identity not be a negative factor, but at times it can be a positive factor in achieving unity among many different types of people. This idea is very controversial, and including lesbians and gay men causes even greater controversy. Such controversy assumes legal dimensions when an organization's mandate of diversity is challenged in court by those who oppose it. For example, a policy that promotes diversity among employees is subject to challenges by unsuccessful applicants who claim they were not hired because they did not belong to a certain group and thus were discriminated against. More specifically, a diversity mandate including lesbians and gay men may be challenged by employees arguing that they are being discriminated against by being forced to work with people whom they find objectionable. While there has not yet been much litigation on diversity questions, many people believe it will occur in the near future. Such litigation has the potential to change the entire landscape of discrimination doctrine, as well as the legal significance of being lesbian, gay, or bisexual.

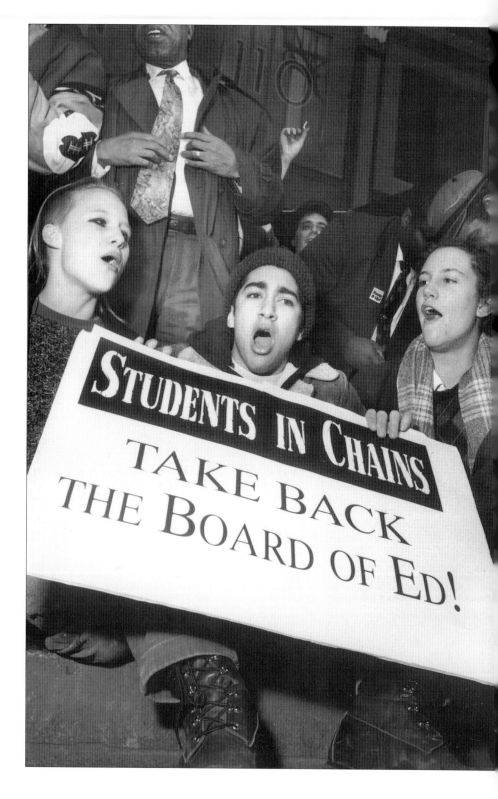

3

Educational Issues

EDUCATIONAL INSTITUTIONS AT ALL levels have been sites of tremendous battles over issues of sexuality. These battles have been over lesbian, gay, bisexual, and transsexual teachers and other educators; the books in school libraries; the curriculum; extracurricular activities; and support for lesbian and gay students and their organizations, including their efforts to promote non-discrimination.

The most long-standing of these controversies is employment discrimination against lesbian, gay, bisexual, and transsexual educators. At one time, schools routinely fired any teacher suspected of being a sexual minority. Likewise, states routinely revoked the teaching licenses of sexual minorities. These actions were generally based upon the requirement that teachers conduct themselves in a moral and professional manner. The label "homosexual" was conclusive proof that a teacher was neither moral nor professional.

Standing up for tolerance can sometimes be lonely, as Kristina Roberson of Bremerton High School in Seattle learned in June 1993. Roberson marched as a contingent of one from Bremerton High in the city's Queer Pride Parade.

Beginning in the late 1960s, however, courts began to seriously consider challenges to dismissals and license revocations. One challenge was that suspicion of homosexuality was not a sufficient basis for a finding of immorality or unprofessionalism. In one of the earliest cases, *Morrison v. State Board of Education,* decided by the California Supreme Court in 1969, the court held that in order to revoke the license of a teacher, there must be some proof that the teacher actually engaged in conduct that rendered him or her unfit to teach. A mere suspicion or even an isolated incident of homosexual activity might not necessarily constitute immorality or unprofessionalism. While the court carefully noted that it was not saying that "homosexuals must be permitted to teach," its conclusion that there must be individual unfitness was nevertheless an advancement. There were also setbacks, however. In other states, courts continued to conclude that homosexuality in and of itself was a sufficient reason to discharge a teacher. In California, subsequent opinions limited the principle of *Morrison* to cases in which there was no sexual conduct. Such limits were insufficient for conservatives, however, who sought to change the law by voter initiative. The Briggs Initiative in 1978 (named after the conservative legislator who authored it) required discharge of any school employee who advocated gay rights. The gay and lesbian community mobilized against the initative, resulting in California voters defeating it, but the Briggs Initiative served as a model for other states.

Oklahoma's statute modeled on the Briggs Initiative was attacked on constitutional grounds. As in all discrimination cases involving governmental organizations, the equal protection clause of the 14th Amendment is important. In cases involving educational institutions, however, the First Amendment is even more important. The First Amendment rights of free association and free speech are raised in many types of discrimination cases, including those involving the military, but the First Amendment has special force in academic cases. Unlike the military, which is an organization based upon discipline, educational institutions are based upon free thought and inquiry, often called academic freedom. This freedom supports an especially expansive reading of the First Amendment in the context of education. Further, when citizens are involved in political speech, such as advocating a change in laws, this speech is entitled to great protection. For example, in the Oklahoma case, although there was not unanimous agreement by the judges who considered the issue, their conclusion was that the statute mandating termination of school employees who advocated gay rights was unconstitutional.

Nevertheless, the First Amendment has not been used to protect lesbian, gay, and bisexual educators in all cases. Among the most distressing cases is that of Marjorie Rowland, a guidance counselor for the Mad River School District in Ohio. In 1974, during her first year on the job, she revealed to one of her colleagues that she was in love, that the object of her love was another woman, and that she was bisexual. Despite Rowland's request, the colleague did not keep this information confidential and informed the school principal. Thereafter, the principal recommended that Rowland's contract not be renewed. Unlike a teacher or other permanent employee, Rowland was not protected by state laws that required a finding of immorality, unprofessionalism, or unfitness for dismissal. But Rowland was protected by the federal constitution. She argued that her termination denied her equal protection because it was based solely on her being bisexual. She also argued that her termination violated the First Amendment because it was based upon her speaking about her love life and upon her private associations. Rowland's case twisted through the federal courts for many years, but it was finally determined that her termination was justified. Ten years after she told a colleague about her new love, the United States Supreme Court refused to hear her case. Although the Court receives requests to hear thousands of cases each year and refuses most of them, Justice William Brennan dissented from the Court's decision. Joined in his opinion by Justice Thurgood Marshall, Brennan wrote that "discrimination against homosexuals or bisexuals based solely on their sexual preference raises significant constitutional questions" and expressed "serious" doubts whether the dismissal of Rowland was constitutional. The Court should hear the case, he decided.

The Court's failure to hear the case was considered a defeat for lesbian, gay, and bisexual educators. Courts continue to rely upon this case to deny constitutional rights to school employees. Discrimination against lesbian, gay, and bisexual educators is justified by the idea that such people can influence students. One of the most damaging pieces of evidence against Rowland was that she counseled two students who revealed that they were bisexual and that she revealed her own sexual orientation to them. While this may seem to be exactly what a guidance counselor should do, the school district argued that this made her job performance unsatisfactory. Lesbian, gay, and bisexual educators are subject to being sued by parents who believe teachers have influenced students. In several cases, high school students have had relationships of varying degrees of intensity with teachers, coaches, and counselors. Such relationships have provoked parents to sue the individual educator as well as the school and school board, usually under theories of "mental distress" or "negligence."

Some parents are also concerned about how the curriculum can influence students. Again, there is seemingly nothing wrong with this because the role of education is to expose students to ideas. Nevertheless, there is much disagreement about exposing students to the possibilities of lesbian, gay, or bisexual lives. Many of these disagreements have legal ramifications. There are many rules, procedures, and laws that govern decisions about curricula. Some localities give teachers wide discretion in deciding what shall be taught, while others vest ultimate discretion in a superintendent of schools. Local school districts also vary in terms of the procedures for selecting school board members and their authority over curriculum decisions. States differ in what in the curriculum is state-mandated and what is decided by local school districts. Disagreements about curricula have been volatile, often centering on lesbian and gay sexuality, but also involving sexuality of any kind. For example, a book is just as likely to be removed from the curriculum or the school library for containing references to heterosexual sexual expression as it is for references to lesbian and gay sexual expression.

When disagreements about curriculum are litigated, the arguments assume constitutional dimensions. As in other situations, both sides argue that their constitutional rights are being violated. When an educational institution removes lesbian and gay material from its curriculum, those who favor its inclusion argue that First Amendment rights of freedom of expression are being infringed. One example of such a controversy is the "Tolerance Day" case of *Solmitz v. Maine School Administrative District No. 59*. Solmitz was a social studies teacher who helped plan Tolerance Day at his high school. As a part of this day, he invited a local lesbian activist to speak about lesbian and gay issues. The principal and school superintendent disapproved because they thought including a lesbian would be too controversial. In fact, some parents protested and there were bomb threats. As a result, the school board canceled Tolerance Day because of worries over security. The social studies teacher and a student sued, arguing that their First Amendment rights relating to academic freedom had been infringed. The case reached Maine's highest court, which held that the school board had discretion to cancel the program as a safety measure. The court carefully noted that the school board had chosen to cancel the entire program and not simply exclude the lesbian speaker.

On the other hand, when an educational institution includes lesbian and gay material in its curriculum, those who object to its inclusion also argue that the school board is infringing First Amendment rights by imposing certain ideas. Those who object to the inclusion of lesbian and gay material may also argue that the school board is infringing First Amendment rights to freedom of religion because tolerance of homosexuality is in opposition to their religious beliefs. Such arguments have usually resulted in "opt out" procedures for parents who do not want their children educated about sexual matters.

While curriculum is the formal part of education, extracurricular activities also comprise an important part of education. Such extracurricular activities can be the foundation for one's academic success. For example, sports can be an important source of funding for higher education, as many students earn college athletic scholarships. For female athletes, gender stereotypes of physically accomplished women as masculine have raised anxieties about lesbianism. One case, *Yost v. Board of Regents,* involved a female student awarded an athletic scholarship in field hockey at the University of Maryland. She sued the university and her coaches for their interference with her First Amendment rights to express her lesbian identity. She argued that because the athletic department determined that "an image of heterosexuality" was best, they ordered her not to be seen with her girlfriend, made derogatory remarks to her, and prohibited her from joining the Lesbian Speakers Bureau or being seen at lesbian and gay events. She was threatened with the loss of her scholarship if she did not abide by these prohibitions. Yost did not sue until she left the university, and thus her lawsuit was complicated by procedural issues concerning its timing and was never fully litigated. Nevertheless, Yost's claims demonstrate the possible ways in which First Amendment protections might be claimed for lesbian and gay athletes.

The mandate of heterosexuality does not only occur in sports. A classic example is the high school prom. The refusal of high school administrators to allow a student to bring an escort of the same sex is often predicated upon the expressed desire (interpreted by some as an excuse) to protect lesbian, gay, or bisexual students from peer violence. In considering a constitutional challenge to such a situation, courts have stressed that prom attendance is "symbolic speech," much like marching in a parade, and thus merits a First Amendment analysis. Under such an analysis, the governmental agency seeking to restrict speech must explore alternatives. In a case that attracted much attention, the court

Today, the question of whether textbooks and other curriculum materials should explicitly incorporate material about gay and lesbian individuals as well as unbiased information regarding health, political, cultural, and social issues related to homosexuality is more widely debated than ever before. These members of the Gay and Lesbian Alliance Against Defamation petitioned the California School Board to include such material in 1990.

in *Fricke v. Lynch* considered a claim by the school that it wanted only to protect the gay students.

Aaron Fricke wanted to bring his friend Paul Guilbert to the Cumberland High School senior prom. The principal, Richard Lynch, denied the request, explaining in a letter to Aaron's parents that the denial was based upon "the real and present threat of physical harm" to Aaron, Aaron's "male escort," and others. There had, in fact, been previous harassment of Aaron's date, Paul. The trial judge believed that Lynch's actions as principal of the high school were sincerely motivated by concern for Aaron and Paul. Nevertheless, the Rhode Island court ruled that although the high school had an important interest in student safety, it should insure safety by more security rather than by excluding Fricke and Guilbert. In recent years, many high school students have organized alternative proms that do not require opposite-sex couples, or even couples at all.

If a school denies funding or other support to an alternative dance or extracurricular activity because it involves lesbian, gay, or bisexual students, this denial also raises constitutional issues. Many student groups have instituted successful lawsuits challenging the denial of funding or recognition to lesbian and gay organizations. For example, students at the University of Arkansas eventually prevailed after their gay and lesbian group was denied funding. The students argued that such a denial infringed their right of free expression. As the federal appellate court in *Gay and Lesbian Law Students v. Gohn* succinctly stated, "a public body that chooses to fund speech or expression must do so even-handedly, without discriminating among recipients on the basis of their ideology." The court noted that the college had no obligation to fund any student organization, but once it decided to fund some, it must fund without regard to the ideas being expressed. Similar earlier litigation involved recognition for the gay and lesbian student group at the University of Missouri, recognition being a prerequisite to apply for funding or use of facilities. In Arkansas and Missouri as well as in many other states students challenged not only their fellow students and school administrators but also the state legislatures. Because state legislatures fund state universities, the funding of gay and lesbian student organizations attracts political attention. Despite opposition from some state lawmakers who have attempted to pass laws limiting funding for "homosexuality," gay, lesbian, and bisexual students have prevailed under the First Amendment.

As always, however, the First Amendment is not only available to gays, lesbians, bisexuals, or other members of minority groups. Persons protesting the funding of lesbian and gay student organizations argue that funding such groups infringes upon the rights of persons who disapprove of homosexuality. For example, some students argued that a mandatory student activities fee assessed by the University of California and used to fund student groups, including the Gay and Lesbian Union, violated their First Amendment rights by forcing them to support ideas that they found objectionable. A court found that since the student activities fee funded many groups and did not deny funding to any group on the basis of ideology, no First Amendment violations occurred.

But like all constitutional requirements, the First Amendment only applies to governmental actions and actors. For example, a court has held that the First Amendment does not apply to a university newspaper. The *Daily Nebraskan,* a campus publication, refused an advertisement seeking a "lesbian roommate" on the grounds that its publication would subject the student placing the ad to a "risk of harassment." As happens so often, the refusal to allow space for lesbian and gay speech was predicated on a desire to protect the speaker. In this case the court found that the newspaper was not sufficiently governmental. Although it was certainly associated with the University of Nebraska, it was nevertheless independent. Thus, the students had no First Amendment rights with regard to the campus newspaper, even though the campus was part of a government-run university.

When educational institutions are not governmental, as in the case of private schools, colleges, and universities, the First Amendment is not applicable to gay, lesbian, and bisexual student groups seeking recognition, funding, or other support from the institution. In such situations, some student groups have relied upon state or local laws that prohibit discrimination on the basis of sexual orientation. Again,

*Emma Kramer Wheeler,
a lesbian high school student
in Brooklyn, New York, spoke
to the press in favor of New York
City's Rainbow Curriculum in
December 1992. Supporters of
the program and others like it
argue that they encourage
tolerance and respect for diversity.*

however, private institutions have argued that if the courts agree with
the students, the government would be interfering with the First
Amendment rights of private institutions. This argument has been
especially successful for schools with a religious affiliation. For example,
the Gay Rights Coalition at Georgetown University, a Jesuit institution,
was involved in a lengthy lawsuit. The students relied upon the District
of Columbia's antidiscrimination ordinance, while the university relied
upon the First Amendment's guarantee of freedom of religion. The
university argued that the endorsement of homosexuality conflicted

with its religious beliefs. The court had a very difficult time with these issues but finally reached a compromise position based upon various interpretations of "endorsement," "recognition," and tangible support for the student group. This position had the practical effect of recognizing the Gay Rights Coalition. After the United States Supreme Court decided it would not grant the university's request to hear the case, the university reached an out-of-court settlement with the students that allowed the organization to exist.

State and local laws against sexual-orientation discrimination have also affected educational institutions' employment placement policies. Many high schools, colleges, and universities allow employers to use school facilities to recruit and interview student applicants. When the employer is the United States military, which specifically prohibits the employment of lesbians and gay men, educational institutions have had to interpret their own duty not to discriminate. Several law student groups have brought successful suits preventing the military from using law-school placement facilities. Courts have ruled that state and local laws prohibiting discrimination apply to military recruitment. Thus, an educational institution subject to a sexual-orientation nondiscrimination law cannot allow the military to use its facilities to recruit as long as the military continues to discriminate on the basis of sexual orientation. The highest court in New York has similarly held that a local school board can exclude the military from recruiting at public schools. In *Lloyd v. Grella,* the court upheld the Rochester City School Board's resolution prohibiting recruitment at schools by all employers, including the military, that discriminated on the basis of sexual orientation. The Rochester example demonstrates the potential for local school boards to fight discrimination against lesbians and gay men.

The Rochester case also contains a factor underlying many education cases, especially those not involving colleges and universities. The Rochester School Board's resolution was not challenged by students or teachers, but by a high school student's parent. The role of parents and ideas about family have a major impact on a number of issues affecting lesbians, gay men, and bisexuals.

4

Families

MOST PEOPLE CONSIDER FAMILIES the major social organization of industrial society. However, people do not agree on what family means or should mean. The law likewise does not have a single definition of family. In the United States, family law (also called domestic relations) is generally governed by state rather than federal laws. This means that each state can develop its own definitions of family, as well as its own rules regulating family matters. Marriage and divorce laws, for example, vary from state to state. Not only are there differences between the states, but there may be differences within a single state's laws. For example, a state's laws may interpret family narrowly when zoning an area for single-family housing and broadly in welfare fraud prosecutions for unreported family income.

Although primary responsibility for laws regarding family lies with the state, the federal government also regulates family. The federal statutes contain over

The inability of gay men and lesbians to obtain legal sanction for long-term domestic partnerships and familial arrangements can have profound consequences.

2,000 references to family, including many in the income tax code and social welfare laws, as well as in laws concerning immigration, education, student loans, highway safety, agriculture, and national security. These laws, as well as the thousands of laws in each state, demonstrate the important position of family in the law.

Given its importance in statutory law, it is perhaps not surprising that the family is generally entitled to constitutional protection. Although "family" is not a term used in the United States Constitution, courts interpreting the Constitution have declared that there is a zone of privacy protecting the family from government intrusion. Like "family," "privacy" does not appear in the Constitution; courts have interpreted the due process clause of the Fifth Amendment (pertaining to the federal government) and the 14th Amendment (pertaining to state governments) to include this idea of familial privacy, often called family autonomy. This autonomy, when expanded to include individual privacy, is the same constitutional principle used to challenge laws regulating sexual expression.

Yet the nature of the constitutional protection for family is somewhat paradoxical. Two principles coexist: the notion that the family unit is of such interest to society as to justify its immense regulation by both federal and state law and the idea that the family exists within a zone of privacy that should be free from government intervention. The interplay of these two principles is especially important in issues concerning gay, lesbian, bisexual, and transgendered youth who come into conflict with disapproving parents.

Parental rights are the best-established constitutional rights regarding family privacy. This constitutional doctrine is traced to *Meyer v. Nebraska* and *Pierce v. Society of Sisters,* two cases that reached the United States Supreme Court during the 1920s. Both of these cases involved conflicts between parents and state regulations regarding the education of children. In *Meyer,* the state of Nebraska had passed a statute that prohibited the teaching of any modern language except English at any public or private grammar school. The passing of this statute was based upon anti-German sentiment during World War I, although it bears a striking similarity to contemporary English-only policies. In *Pierce,* the state of Oregon had passed a statute making education at public schools compulsory. This statute meant that education at private and parochial schools was insufficient to comply with state law. In both these cases, the Supreme Court held that the state statutes were unconstitutional because they infringed upon the rights of the parents to direct and control the upbringing of their children. Although the Court did not explicitly say so, its decision is consistent with common–law traditions that view children as property, especially of their fathers. It is also consistent with current law: until persons are 18 or otherwise emancipated (usually indicated by living apart from their parents and being financially independent or married), they are minors with incomplete legal status and lesser constitutional rights.

For all youth, being subject to the direction and control of parents or guardians can cause problems. For lesbian, gay, bisexual, and transgendered youth, these problems are often intensified by parental confusion, anxiety, or hostility toward sexual difference. In accordance with their constitutional right to direct and control the upbringing of their children, some parents have sought to have their children "educated" into a traditional model of heterosexuality. This "education" can include involuntary commitment to psychiatric institutions. One estimate is that more than 48,000 young people are signed into institutions each year by their parents or otherwise involuntarily committed. A disproportionate number of these young people are lesbian, gay, bisexual, or transgendered. Some of the diagnoses supporting psychiatric commitments may explain this disproportionate number. "Adolescent conduct disorders" are diagnosed when a youth opposes a parent, an obvious outcome in a situation in which a parent is hostile to a child's sexual development. "Borderline personality disorder" includes the symptom of "confusion over sexual identity." "Gender identity disorder" applies to youth who exhibit "discomfort" with their assigned identity of male or female. For lesbian, gay, bisexual, and transgendered youth, such "diagnoses" make psychiatric problems of daily existence.

Once institutionalized, a youth is subject to therapy. At some institutions, the treatment can be less than rigorous, consisting mostly of supervision. However, even this minimal supervision occurs in a climate hostile to lesbian, gay, bisexual, and transgendered existence. Many of the workers, including the psychiatrists, may believe that heterosexuality is the only correct sexual orientation. At other institutions, the treatment is more invasive. There have been reported instances of "reparative" treatments that attempt to "reorient" the youth to heterosexuality. In some instances, this occurs through forcing the youth to submit to sexual encounters with a person of the opposite sex.

Such forced heterosexual encounters—some might term them rape—have a long history in the treatment of lesbian, gay, bisexual, and

The activist group Queer Nation organized this public marriage ceremony inside San Francisco's City Hall in September 1990 to protest the state of California's continued refusal to allow same-sex marriages.

transgendered persons. At times, the law has intervened by disapproving such "treatments" for adults. For example, *Hartogs v. Employers Mutual* concerns a lawsuit by a lesbian against her psychiatrist for medical malpractice. Over a 13-month period beginning in 1971, the psychiatrist prescribed and personally administered "fornication therapy" to cure the patient's lesbianism. The jury awarded the lesbian over $150,000, an especially large sum for the time. Almost as important legally, the court upheld the insurance agency's refusal to be responsible for the psychiatrist's actions. Although the insurance policy covered

medical malpractice, the insurance company argued and the court agreed that the treatment was not medical at all (although the lesbian patient believed it was) but a violation of professional ethics. However, the American Psychiatric Association has not banned as unethical therapies that seek to change sexual orientation even when such therapies include sexual encounters. The legal landscape is likewise murky, despite cases such as *Hartogs*. For youth, this murkiness is compounded by their nonadult status.

The situation of lesbian, gay, bisexual, and transgendered youth is beginning to attract the attention of legal advocates. Attorney Shannon Minter at the National Center for Lesbian Rights has established a program offering legal support for any youth confronting problems with mental-health care because of her or his sexual orientation or gender identity. The project seeks to legally prevent involuntary commitment or involuntary submission to reparative therapies, meaning that the youth rather than the parent has to agree.

The ability to advocate on behalf of a youth and against a parent's desires is possible because the constitutional right of parents to "direct and control" the upbringing of their children is not unlimited. The state can interfere for numerous reasons, especially if a child is considered to be in danger. In such cases, the state is considered *parens patriae*—standing in the shoes of the parent—so it can assert the interests of the child against the biological, adoptive, or other legal parents or guardians. Thus, every state has a statutory scheme—sometimes termed dependency—for interfering with families in cases of abuse or neglect. In these cases, if a court concludes the statutory requirements are met, the state can relocate a child to another relative, to foster care, or to an institution, or the state may allow the parent to retain custody but place conditions on the parent. Generally, such proceedings must be brought by the state, usually in the person of a social worker employed by a state social-services agency. Recently, however, courts have begun to recognize cases brought by the children themselves. In the widely publicized cases of children "divorcing" their parents, courts have allowed minors to bring abuse and neglect actions against their parents.

Parents can also abdicate responsibility for their children in favor of the state. While there are many cases of "throwaway" lesbian, gay, bisexual, and transgendered youth that occur informally, many states permit parents to accomplish it through formal legal procedures. States having persons-in-need-of-supervision statutes allow a parent or legal guardian to voluntarily relinquish custody of the child to the state. The court need only conclude that the parent cannot control or supervise the minor. The minor then becomes a ward of the state and is usually placed in foster care or in a state institution. Unlike a juvenile delinquency proceeding, there are few procedural protections for the minor because no crime is involved. Whether the case is brought by a state agency, the child, or the parent, if the fate of the minor is the ultimate issue, it is a civil proceeding, usually taking place in family court. There might—or might not—be criminal prosecution of the parents for abuse, but this is exceedingly rare. The vast majority of the thousands of abuse, neglect, and related cases heard by courts every week are civil proceedings.

Family law also affects people over 18 years of age. Interestingly, even for lesbian, gay, bisexual, and transgendered adults, the issues may involve their parents. The continuing involvement of parents is caused by the law's limited definition of family. In traditional law, a person's family is her or his parents, until she or he enters into a heterosexual marriage. The absence of such a marriage means that one's parents remain one's legal family. This is true even if one had no contact with one's parents for many years. In most situations, the legal definition of family has no importance. In other cases, however, it has the power to negate lesbian and gay relationships.

One of the most devastating of such situations has been that of Sharon Kowalski and Karen Thompson. In November 1983, Kowalski was in a car accident and suffered extensive injuries limiting her ability to communicate. Until her accident, she had been living with her lover, Thompson, in a house they were buying together. After her accident, Kowalski was not self-sufficient, and the question who would be responsible for her care arose. Although she and Thompson had exchanged rings and considered their relationship a "life partnership

These two happy couples were among the first to take advantage of a local ordinance passed by the city of San Francisco in 1991 that allowed same-sex couples to register their domestic partnerships. Other than legal recognition, however, the ordinance conferred no tangible legal benefits.

. . . similar to a marriage," they were legal strangers. Kowalski's legal family consisted of her parents, who did not believe that their daughter was a lesbian or could be involved in a lesbian relationship with anyone, including Thompson. Because Kowalski had been incapacitated—judged legally "incompetent"—her legal status was more like that of a child than of an adult. Thus, she needed a legal guardian. Because the appointment of a legal guardian generally reflects the law's definition of family, Kowalski's parents—and not her lover—were the obvious legal choice. If the law appointed Kowalski's parents guardians, they not only could control her finances and medical treatment choices but also could determine where she would live and who could visit her. The prospect of not being allowed to even visit her lover prompted Thompson to bring an action in court. In one of the many papers filed in the litigation, a doctor testifying on behalf of Kowalski's parents stated that "visits by Karen Thompson would expose Sharon Kowalski to a high risk of sexual abuse."

Such homophobic statements, coupled with the feelings of many lesbians and gay men that they were only a car accident away from a similar situation, contributed to the attention the case attracted. Lesbian, gay, bisexual, feminist, and disabled persons activists focused considerable energies on the litigation.

The history of the case, which lasted for eight years, is illuminating. Despite the fact that Kowalski's parents finally withdrew their claim to be their daughter's guardian, the judge refused to name Thompson as guardian. The trial judge expressed concern that Kowalski's parents still objected to Thompson as guardian (in part on the basis of her lesbianism), that Thompson had been involved with at least one other woman in the years since Kowalski's 1983 accident, and that Thompson had invaded Kowalski's privacy by revealing her sexual orientation to her parents and by taking her to lesbian and gay gatherings. Rather than naming Thompson as guardian, the judge named a supposedly neutral third party, a legal stranger but not Kowalski's lesbian lover.

An appellate court reversed the trial judge's decision. The court relied on the uncontroverted medical testimony that Kowalski had sufficient capacity to choose her guardian and that she had consistently chosen Thompson. The court also noted that Thompson was "the only person willing to take care of Sharon Kowalski outside of an institution." In a phrase that the lesbian and gay press reiterated in tones of victory, the appellate court also confirmed the trial court's finding that Kowalski and Thompson were a "family of affinity which should be accorded respect." This respect conveniently coincides in this instance with preventing Kowalski from becoming financially dependent on the state for institutional care.

Prompted at least in part by the protracted litigation of the Kowalski case, lesbian and gay legal reformers have developed strategies to make the law more hospitable to daily needs. These strategies include both working within the present laws as well as trying to change the law. Thus, one suggestion is the use of durable powers of attorney, so that Kowalski could have named Thompson as her guardian in the event of her incapacitation. Like all legal documents, a power of attorney is not foolproof, but courts are generally enforcing these individual attempts to redefine family. Another suggestion has been to legalize same-sex marriage, so that Thompson would have been recognized as Kowalski's "next of kin," just as if she had been a husband or wife. State laws regulating marriage generally require one person of each sex. Often the statutes do not explicitly mention this requirement, but merely imply it with language like "the man" and "the woman." Courts interpreting these statutes have concluded that the requirements of one person of each sex—no more, no less—are clear from the statutes and "common sense."

Many legal theorists believe that the current restrictions on same-sex marriage parallel past restrictions on racial intermarriage. At one time, many states enforced laws that prohibited nonwhites from marrying whites. Such laws were not declared unconstitutional by the United States Supreme Court until *Loving v. Virginia* in 1967. Lesbians and gay men who have litigated their right to marry have relied upon this case to challenge laws that prohibit same-sex marriages. The handful of appellate courts that have considered this claim have generally decided that laws limiting marriage to pairs of opposite-sex couples are constitutionally valid. Courts find no violation of equality doctrine because homosexuals are not a class entitled to heightened protection and the state laws are rational. Litigants who raise the possibility of gender and sexual-orientation discrimination are told that there is no gender discrimination because women cannot marry women and men cannot marry men; there would only be gender discrimination if men could marry men but women could not marry women (or vice versa). One exception has been the well-publicized decision by a state court in Hawaii that held there to be "sex" discrimination in prohibiting same-sex marriage, but the impact of this decision remains uncertain.

Legal marriage could have numerous benefits for those lesbians and gay men in couple relationships. There are economic benefits such as certain tax considerations; extra social security, workers' compensation, and other public benefits; mutual health-insurance coverage and other private employer benefits; immigration preference; and inclusion in housing regulations. Further, if a couple is legally married, there would be little need to provide for one's lover by using the tools previously discussed because the operative laws would favor the lesbian "spouse." However, there might also be many practical disadvantages for a couple, depending on their circumstances, including increased tax liability, decreased financial aid such as public assistance, and the costs of divorce if the relationship ended.

Practical advantages and disadvantages are not all that are at stake in legalized same-sex marriage. The law has symbolic as well as practical value. Lesbians, gay men, bisexuals, and transgendered persons disagree about what the law should symbolize about their relationships. These disagreements have basically split into two camps. On one side, there are those who argue that gay and lesbian relationships are "just like" heterosexual ones, thus advocating that marriage be extended to same-gender couples and meanwhile pushing for various reforms, including domestic-partnership policies. On the other side, there are those who insist that gay and lesbian relationships are "different" from traditional heterosexual ones, and who thus seek broader reforms that would not link economic or other benefits to relationships. In a practical context, those in the "just like" camp argue that it is unfair that a married woman might be able to obtain health insurance or other benefits for her husband while a lesbian (denied the legal state of marriage) cannot obtain those same benefits. Those in the "different" camp argue that what is unfair is the fact that anyone's health insurance depends upon maintaining a relationship with someone employed by a corporation that provides health benefits. In the political context, those in the "just like" camp are often derided as assimilationists or naive Pollyannas who believe that the institution of marriage and the domination of hetero-sexuals will be dismantled the day same-sex marriage is legalized. Those in the "different" camp are also derided: they are politically correct radicals who believe that monogamy, couples, home ownership, and probably even the law are bad. Because the "assimilationist" and "separatist" camps are essentially political divisions, which are further complicated by considerations such as race, class, age, and ability, a consensus stance on marriage is as unlikely as a consensus on any other political issue.

Nevertheless, some advocates are pursuing other avenues to obtain the practical benefits of marriage. At one time, adoption—one partner adopting the other—was an option, but this has generally been discredited because the legal relationship created is one that replicates parent and child. Another much more popular and recent avenue is "domestic partnership." This is available by ordinance in some cities and municipalities and by policy from some employers, notably universities and large or progressive corporations, and is becoming more common. A domestic partnership entitles the partners to certain benefits, most typically health insurance or other spouse-of-employee benefits such as leave, pension, or family housing. Affidavits required under domestic partnership ordinances or policies typically require a sworn affirmation that the relationship meets criteria associated with traditional marriage: there must be exclusivity ("I swear this is my one and only domestic partner"), economic interdependency (joint bank accounts), and shared living quarters, sometimes for a mandated period of time ("We have occupied the same residence, exclusively and continuously, for longer than the previous three months"). Such affidavits can usually be withdrawn by filing another affidavit.

Another avenue to achieve some of the benefits of marriage has been specific litigation to have a regulation or policy referring to a "spouse" or "family member" be interpreted to include one's partner. Such litigation has had mixed success. For example, it was successful in forestalling an eviction based upon a regulation that allowed only surviving "family members" to remain in a rent-stabilized apartment after the named tenant's death, but it was not successful in allowing a lover not named as a beneficiary in a will to claim the share entitled to a spouse who has been disinherited. In both cases, surviving lovers of men who had died from acquired immunodeficiency syndrome (AIDS) sought the benefits to which they would have been entitled had they been legally recognized spouses. The criteria generally employed by the courts are the characteristics of traditional heterosexual marriage, including economic interdependency, cohabitation, and exclusivity.

In addition to relationships with parents and partners, our relationships with children are also governed by family law. Even more than legal doctrine regarding partners, the law regarding child custody is rapidly changing. Child custody can involve a dispute between parents during a divorce, a dispute between a parent and another relative, a dispute between a parent and the state as in an abuse and neglect

Pushing empty baby strollers as a symbolic gesture, demonstrators marched around the Virginia Supreme Court Building in the city of Richmond in September 1993 to protest a judge's decision to take the two-year-old son of Sharon Bottoms from his mother's custody because her lesbianism made her an unfit parent. No grounds other than Bottoms's sexual orientation were cited as demonstration of her alleged unfitness.

proceeding, a dispute between lesbian or gay coparents who are terminating their relationship, or a dispute between the parties responsible for the conception of the child.

A dispute between parents during a divorce is the most common type of child custody dispute. All states adhere to the legal standard of awarding custody in the "best interests of the child." This is obviously a very vague, broad, and discretionary standard. A judge considers numerous factors depending upon the particular state statute or case law. The ultimate goal is to weigh the relative merits of each parent in terms of the child's best interests. Factors considered include economic, educational, social, and cultural ones, and sometimes the child's preference. Some commentators have argued that the best interests of the child really means the best interests of the government. Judges often reason that a child who grows up in a conventional family will be a better citizen.

The fact that one parent is lesbian, gay, bisexual, or transgendered is a factor that all courts consider. There are three different approaches that the courts can take. The first and most limiting is that living with a homosexual parent cannot be in the child's best interests; the other parent is awarded custody. The second or middle approach is that living with a homosexual parent can be in the child's best interests as long as the parent is a parent first. Under this approach, courts disapprove of lesbians or gay men who "flaunt it" or engage in lesbian and gay politics, or sometimes even live with a lover. The third and presumably most enlightened approach is the "nexus" approach. Courts use what they call the nexus test to determine whether the parent's sexual orientation actually harms the child. In practice, the application of this harm principle can make the nexus test indistinguishable from the first two approaches.

The types of harm that courts often consider under this nexus test include the harm of exposure to molestation; the harm of stigmatization to the child because of having a gay or lesbian parent; and the harm of living in an immoral and illegal environment. Courts have also considered the harm of a potential gay or lesbian identity in the child, implicitly reasoning that it is not in the best interest of any child to be lesbian, gay, bisexual, or transgendered. Yet not all courts agree. Many courts, including appellate courts in New Jersey, Alaska, Massachusetts, South Carolina, and New York have specifically found that a parent's gay or lesbian identity did not constitute a harm to the child. However, underlying even these relatively liberal opinions is the assumption that having a lesbian or gay parent could be more harmful to a child than having a heterosexual parent and thus would not be in the child's best interest.

A lesbian or gay parent's custody of a child can also be challenged by third parties. These third parties—not one of the child's two parents—typically include the child's grandparents or other relatives. These third parties do not have a claim of custody equal to the parent's claim. Rather than applying a pure best interest test, courts require the third party to show some extraordinary circumstances that would justify denying the parent custody. Such extraordinary circumstances include parental unfitness. In some cases, courts have held that a parent's lesbian or gay identity itself demonstrates unfitness. One such case was that of Sharon Bottoms and her two-year-old son, Tyler. This case attracted nationwide attention in 1993 when a judge in Virginia awarded custody of Tyler to his maternal grandmother. The grandmother had sought custody of Tyler by arguing that her daughter's lesbian relationship made her an unfit parent. Interestingly, the grandmother's lawsuit occurred after Bottoms objected to Tyler's visiting the grandmother's home, which would expose him to a man who had sexually abused Bottoms as she was growing up. Nevertheless, the trial judge found that Tyler belonged with his grandmother rather than his lesbian mother. He based part of his opinion on Virginia's sodomy law, reasoning that Bottoms's violation of this law rendered her an unfit parent.

The judge's decision provoked an outpouring of protest. Many lesbian and gay legal advocates participated in appealing the decision to a Virginia appellate court. This court reversed the earlier decision, concluding that Bottoms—not her mother—should have custody of Tyler. The appellate court stated that Bottoms's lesbianism did not render her an unfit parent, absent any specific showing that her sexual orientation was harming Tyler.

While Bottoms was successful in regaining custody of her son, many other lesbian and gay parents are not. One tragic situation is that of Andrea White. In 1990, the Supreme Court of Mississippi affirmed an award of custody of her children to their paternal grandparents. Mississippi's highest court noted disapprovingly that the trial judge "relied almost exclusively" on the mother's lesbian relationship to deny her custody. But rather than reverse the trial judge (as the Virginia appellate court did in Bottoms's case), the Mississippi court looked at other evidence. The court considered conflicting testimony about the children being outside in cold weather without adequate clothing. After noting that trial judges have a great degree of discretion in custody matters, the Mississippi Supreme Court upheld the denial of custody to White. The court also upheld a condition of visitation: the children could not visit their mother in the presence of her lover.

Neither Bottoms nor White is a middle-class model of respectability. Both women struggled to raise children in impoverished circumstances, and neither of the fathers contributed any child support. Interestingly, White's financial situation had improved after she separated from her husband and began living with her lesbian lover. No one claimed that the children's father should be awarded custody, "given his financial situation and his drinking problem." Yet when White became involved with a woman, her husband's parents decided that she should not have custody of her children. The courts of Mississippi agreed. Like so many other situations in which gay or lesbian parents lose custody of their children, this one attracted little attention.

Like a third party, the state can also challenge a parent's custody. While state abuse and neglect proceedings may be used to the advantage of lesbian, gay, bisexual, and transgendered youth, these proceedings can also be used to remove children from lesbian, gay, bisexual, and transgendered parents. In *Briesch,* a Pennsylvania case, a mother appealed when the state took away her preschool son, who had a speech problem. The appellate court upheld the removal, noting that "Joey was exposed to a chaotic and harmful home life. The mother is a lesbian who effects a masculine appearance, wears men's clothing, and has a masculine oriented mental status. At the time of the hearing, she lived

In the course of the 1987 March on Washington for Gay and Lesbian Rights, approximately 1,000 same-sex couples were symbolically married in front of the Internal Revenue Service Building. The placard held aloft by a member of one such couple expressed the prevailing sentiment regarding the most crucial ingredient necessary to create a family.

with Nancy M . . . and two of her children in a two bedroom apartment." The court also found the mother "uncooperative" because she took notes in her meetings with a social worker and responded in an "adversarial manner" with references to her attorney. When the mother refused the condition that she not live with her lover, the court found that this "revealed forcefully her true feelings and attitudes regarding Joey's [speech] therapy." The appellate court rejected the mother's claim that the court was unnecessarily interfering in her lesbian relationship because there was no causal connection between her lesbianism and harm to the child. The court noted that the order to exclude the lover from their home was not meant to interfere with the lesbian relationship but only to establish order and encourage a close relationship between mother and son. Thus, the court was able to claim that the mother's lesbianism was irrelevant in its decision. Nevertheless, many believe that such decisions are based upon the parent's sexual orientation despite the court's claims.

Sexual orientation can also become an issue when both parents are lesbian or gay. Many have reported on a "lesbian baby boom" in which great numbers of lesbians have been giving birth. In many instances, a lesbian couple decides to raise the child together, and one woman is inseminated by a donor. If the couple later separates, a legal dispute can arise over custody of the child. Courts most often decide that only the biological mother—the lesbian who carried the child and actually gave birth—has the right to custody. The case of *Alison D. v. Virginia M.* is the best-known example of such a situation. New York courts, including the Court of Appeals, the state's highest, rejected a claim by the lesbian nonbiological mother, Alison D. Her claim was not for custody but only for visitation, and she argued that although she was not a legal parent, she was a de facto parent. The courts basically said that while this might be true, a de facto parent has no legal claims, including visitation rights.

The court noted that Alison D. would have had a claim if she had adopted the child. Such adoptions, often called "second-parent adoptions," are a very new development in the law. These adoptions allow the lesbian or gay partner of a legal parent to adopt the child. Courts have troubled over the legal implications of this procedure because usually an adoption terminates the legal parent's rights. But many courts have analogized these second-parent adoptions to stepparent adoptions and allowed them under the same terms. However, some judges and courts refuse to allow such adoptions, usually because of strict interpretations of the statutes applicable.

Such adoptions also terminate the rights of any other possible parents. In the case of two lesbians, another possible parent is the sperm donor, who is the biological father. In the case of two gay men, it is the biological mother. If a second-parent adoption has not occurred, the sperm donor or biological mother may still have a legal claim. This claim is based upon the traditional biological definition of parent, even though the sperm donor may be a gay man or the biological mother a lesbian. In a few cases, this situation has arisen when a gay male sperm donor has claimed a right to visit or share custody of a child with two lesbian mothers. Courts in these cases have had a difficult time rendering decisions. In one case, after an extended trial, the court concluded that based upon the sperm donor's status as more of a friend of the family than father for the child's first 10 years, he could not now claim the status of father. That finding was recently reversed in a bitterly divided three-to-two decision by an appellate court and is presently being considered by the state's highest court. This case has caused tremendous disagreement in the lesbian, gay, and bisexual legal community, in part because some of the adults involved are attorneys and known to members of the legal community, in part because the dispute involves a gender divide between women and men, and in part because there is no general agreement on suitable models for gay and lesbian families. Underlying many of the disagreements about this case are fundamental disagreements about the meaning and boundaries of "fatherhood" and "parenthood."

Litigation involving lesbian, gay, bisexual, and transgendered families is on the cutting edge of traditional legal circles. Family law professors routinely include several cases involving lesbian and gay issues in their classes. In one survey, one-third of all law students considered lesbian and gay issues to be the most important aspect of family law. Certainly, gay and lesbian families pose a challenge for legal advocates and theorists who ask where these alternative families should fit into the law, if at all. Just as certainly, the law poses a challenge for lesbians, gay men, bisexuals, and transgendered persons who ask how they should shape their relationships to fit the the law, if at all.

5

Criminal Justice

LESBIANS, GAY MEN, BISEXUALS, and transgendered persons can be either victims or perpetrators of crimes. Sometimes they can be involved both as victims and perpetrators, as in cases of domestic violence. Regardless of the role they play, society's prejudices against them can surface.

Lynn Griffis, a newly ordained lesbian minister in one of San Francisco's largest gay churches, shows the mutilation she says was inflicted on her by a group of homophobic skinheads in a 1989 incident. In recent years, the likelihood of gay men and lesbians becoming enmeshed in the criminal justice system as the victims of gay bashing has increased.

In the last few years, there has been an increasing awareness about the extent of violence against lesbians, gay men, bisexuals, and transgendered persons. The murder of Rebecca Wight and attempted murder of Claudia Brenner attracted nationwide attention. Wight and Brenner were camping on the Appalachian Trail when they were assaulted by a barrage of bullets. The assailant, Stephen Roy Carr, reportedly lived in a cave and had stalked them on the trail. He was apprehended and charged with murder. He raised a defense that he was "provoked" to murder because he spied them making love. At one time, such provocation defenses were routinely considered—and sometimes accepted—by juries. The trial judge rejected Carr's defense as a matter of law, so that the jury would not even be able to consider it. The judge also refused to hear evidence about Carr's rejection by women and his mother's lesbianism. Carr waived his right to a jury trial and the judge convicted him of first-degree murder and sentenced him to life imprisonment. Although Carr appealed, the appellate court agreed with the trial judge, noting: "The sight of naked women engaged in lesbian lovemaking is not adequate provocation." Similarly, most courts now reject a defense of being provoked to murder because the victim made homosexual advances, although this so-called homosexual panic defense was entertained by juries for many years.

In addition to recognizing violence against lesbians and gay men as a national problem, many have linked this violence with the violence against others on the basis of group identities such as race, ethnicity, religion, culture, and gender. Much of this awareness is due to the efforts of the Anti-Violence Project of the National Gay & Lesbian Task Force, other national organizations, and many, many local grassroots organizations. Antiviolence projects and independent researchers throughout the United States have been documenting incidents of violence against lesbians and gay men since the early 1980s. This documentation has led to a widespread belief that such violence is a tremendous problem, perhaps even an epidemic.

The government has also begun to collect its own statistics. In 1987, Connecticut became the first state to pass a hate crimes statistics act, although this act provided only the vaguest definitions of "hate crime." In 1990, Congress passed the Hate Crime Statistics Act, which provides for the compilation of statistics of hate or bias crimes, specifically defined as "crimes that manifest evidence of prejudice based upon race, religion, sexual orientation, or ethnicity." The inclusion of sexual orientation as a category was the result of intense lobbying by lesbian and gay activists amidst much controversy within Congress. The compromise necessary to preserve the sexual orientation category included a statement in the act that "the American family is the foundation of American society; federal policy should encourage the well-being, financial security, and

Provoked by a judge's decision to allow defense attorneys to question prospective jurors about their sexual orientation in a 1991 New York City murder trial, activists from Queer Nation, the Gay and Lesbian Anti-Violence Project, and other organizations picket outside the State Supreme Court Building in the borough of Queens. The case was one of several in recent years in which accused murderers have attempted to use the homosexual orientation and alleged aggressive sexual conduct of their victim as a defense for their act.

health of the American family; and schools should not de-emphasize the critical value of American family life." Any doubts that this tribute to the family was meant as an antidote to the mention of sexual orientation is resolved by the statute's next section: "Nothing in this Act shall be construed, nor shall any funds be appropriated to carry out the purpose of the Act be used, to promote or encourage homosexuality." The act also includes a rebuttal to any possible judicial interpretation that a law requiring the collection of statistics about violence based on sexual orientation might mean that discrimination based on it is wrong: "Nothing in this section creates a right to bring an action, including an action based on discrimination due to sexual orientation."

As some legal theorists have noted, it is ironic that an act that seeks to collect statistics about violence implicitly approves of discrimination. Many legal reformers believe that the repeal of statutes criminalizing sex and the passage of statutes preventing discrimination are necessary steps in the quest to end violence against lesbians and gay men. Nevertheless, the act specifically rejects these goals. This irony does not mean that the act is not progress; it does mark the first time the term "sexual orientation" appears in the federal statutes, and the signing of the Hate Crime Statistics Act was the first time openly gay men and lesbians were invited to the White House. But it also means that there remains some legal ambivalence toward a total eradication of violence.

The act's definition of the term "sexual orientation" invites another comparison with discrimination doctrine. The act defines "sexual orientation" as "consensual homosexuality and heterosexuality." Including heterosexuality obscures the dominant status of heterosexuality, so that violence against a heterosexual by a lesbian or gay man would be a hate crime. For example, if a heterosexual man enters a lesbian bar and makes explicit heterosexual advances to the lesbian customers, and the lesbians shove him into the bathroom and lock him in there because they find such flagrant heterosexuality inappropriate and offensive, the lesbians have committed a hate crime, because they manifested "evidence of prejudice" based on the sexual orientation of heterosexuality. Many legal thinkers would distinguish this situation from one in which a group of heterosexuals stalks and beats up gay men or lesbians. These thinkers point not only to a power imbalance on the streets but also in the law itself: the adjective "consensual" modifies "homosexual" but arguably not "heterosexual," as if there are many homosexual encounters without consent but not any heterosexual encounters without consent. Further, there is a valid objection to the omission of bisexuality and transgender in the definition.

Yet the act does make local police more aware of hate crimes. Increasingly, police departments are training officers to make final determinations about whether a suspected bias incident can be confirmed as a bias incident. For example, the New York City Police Department's Bias Incident Investigation Unit has issued guidelines that stress the officer's "common sense" in confirming bias incidents. The guidelines list considerations such as motive, display of offensive symbols, suspects' statements, victims' perceptions, and similarity to previous incidents. The guidelines even note that borderline cases should be resolved in favor of confirmation, although they also warn that "mere mention of a bias remark does not necessarily make an incident bias motivated," again stressing the use of commonsense judgment.

Despite such guidelines, many people in the gay and lesbian community remain suspicious of police officers. This suspicion is based in part on the historic hostility of law enforcement officials to lesbians, gay men, and transgendered persons. There is also some evidence that police officers themselves are sometimes perpetrators of violence against gay men and lesbians.

These governmental efforts to count bias crimes are merely efforts to compile information and acquire data. Those who find this insufficient often advocate the enhancement of penalties for bias crimes or the more rigorous enforcement of criminal laws. These proposals are related to the relatively new term "hate crime." The two component parts of the term hate crime are in tension with each other. On the one hand, hate is usually not against the law. On the other hand, a crime is a crime, regardless of hate. This tension results in two different perspectives: the special and the neutral.

The special model proposes that some crimes are worse than others and should be accorded special recognition. This is the model that looms behind the federal statistics act, allowing for special treatment in the statistical compilation of crimes evidencing hate. The enhancement of penalties proposal is also within this model. Penalty enhancement allows a judge to impose longer prison sentences if it is found that the crime was motivated by prejudice. For example, the New Hampshire statute that allowed judges to impose longer sentences in circumstances such as prior convictions was recently amended to include a hate crime provision: an extended term of imprisonment may be imposed if the defendant "was substantially motivated to commit the crime because of hostility toward the victim's religion, race, creed, sexual orientation, national origin, or sex."

The neutral model suggests that existing criminal laws need to be enforced impartially. This model requires the rigorous enforcement of criminal laws and penalties, no matter who the victim is. It is advanced by lesbian and gay legal reformers protesting against judges who impose lenient sentences or prosecutors who refuse to prosecute crimes com-

Queer Nation demonstrators protest cinematic depictions of gay men and lesbians outside the 1992 Academy Awards ceremony at the Dorothy Chandler Pavilion in Los Angeles. Hollywood has only rarely depicted gay and lesbian individuals as well-adjusted, productive, valuable members of society, and in recent years a number of box-office smashes—notably The Silence of the Lambs *and* Basic Instinct—*have featured gay or lesbian serial killers.*

mitted against lesbians or gay men. A neutral principle is important any time a perpetrator raises a defense based upon the identity of the victim. According to this perspective, what is needed is not special protection but only equal treatment.

Still another approach is based upon a recognition that not all violence is a crime. For example, a person could scream "faggot" or "dyke" at another person repeatedly, but this emotional violence may not be a crime. Given this gap between violence and crime, proposals for the creation of new crimes dealing with intimidation and harassment seek to expand the law's recognition and punishment of the violence against lesbians and gay men. Another proposal is to create or increase civil liability for such acts, so that the victim could sue the perpetrator for money damages.

The creation of a new category of crime or offense, called hate crimes, has occurred mostly in municipalities and on college campuses. The relevant statutes or regulations generally provide punishment for hateful activity, slurs, or epithets indicating bias. Yet because such crimes are often speech or speech acts, such laws are subject to attack under the constitutional free speech doctrine. Evaluating these laws involves balancing governmental interests in preventing hate and individual rights to freedom of speech. But the balance often tilts toward free speech. The United States Supreme Court recently declared unconstitutional an ordinance of St. Paul, Minnesota, that criminalized the placing of symbols, objects, or graffiti known to arouse "anger, alarm, or resentment" on the basis of "race, color, creed, religion, or gender." As in many other hate crime provisions, sexual orientation was omitted, but the case is nevertheless important for future attempts to criminalize hateful acts against lesbians, gay men, bisexuals, and transgendered persons. Courts have reached similar decisions in challenges by some students against university policies that prohibited hate speech. Thus, at this time it seems very difficult to draft a constitutional law or policy that can prohibit verbal violence.

A difficulty of a different sort is posed by situations in which lesbians and gay men are not only the victims but also the perpetrators of crimes. One such situation is violence between intimate partners, often called domestic violence. The recognition of domestic violence has its roots in the battered women's movement. It was the hard work of feminists, many of whom are lesbians, that forced legal reforms on behalf of women battered by their husbands. One reform was the order of protection, a court order that prohibits further abuse and may also include temporary judgments such as excluding the abuser from the home. Another reform was making the battered woman syndrome available as a defense in prosecutions of women who murder their abusers. Yet concrete legal reforms—and even the concept of domestic violence—have not necessarily been extended to lesbian and gay relationships.

For example, although orders of protection are now available in every state, very few states extend such protection to persons in lesbian or gay relationships. Some states, such as Virginia, limit protective orders to spouses. Other states, such as Utah, Louisiana, and Maine, allow protective orders to be used when people are married, have been married, or have a child in common. The state of Missouri takes the unusual position of limiting protective orders to persons of the "opposite sex." In an increasing number of states, including Connecticut, Idaho, Montana, New York, Pennsylvania, and Wisconsin, a protective order may be available for lesbian and gay relationships. In these states, often because of recent amendments, protective order statutes only require "sharing a residence." For lesbians or gay men who have never lived together as a part of their relationship, orders of protection are rarely available.

Yet even where there is a statute allowing for an order of protection, judges may refuse to issue the order for lesbian or gay relationships. Judges often decide that the situation is not battering or abuse but "mutual combat" or simply fighting. Judges often seem uneasy with violence that does not involve a heterosexual relationship. Traditional defenders of battered women are often similarly uncomfortable. In part, this is because the movement against domestic violence is rooted in ideas about men's dominance over women. When a woman dominates another woman or a man dominates another man, the situation may seem unclear. A judge may thus either deny the restraining order or issue a mutual restraining order. Or the judge may fall back on gender stereotypes, trying to determine the more masculine person (who would be the abuser) from the more feminine person (who would be the battered person). Additionally, gender stereotypes of women as being prone to "catfights" or of men who should be able to "fight like a man" influence conceptions of domestic violence in lesbian and gay relationships. The specific issues of lesbian and gay domestic violence are only beginning to receive legal recognition.

Legal recognition of domestic violence in lesbian and gay relationships is important to prevent further violence. The situation of Annette Green is an example. Living in Florida, she was not able to obtain a protective order, which by statute were available in that state only to "persons related by blood or marriage." She was also not able to go to a shelter or obtain services from domestic violence centers, which are partially funded by the state and thus totally regulated by it, because the relevant statute defines domestic violence as violence "by a person against the person's spouse." Because Green sought protection from her lover, there was no legal recourse.

In 1989, a Florida prosecutor charged Green with the murder of her lover, Ivonne Julio. Interestingly, the prosecutor charged Green with first-degree murder, despite such circumstances as struggle in an intimate setting, which usually prompt a lesser degree of murder charge. The prosecutor also objected to the use of a battered woman defense, even while admitting that Green had been "battered. She was shot at before by the victim. She had a broken nose, broken ribs." Despite the prosecutor's objection, the trial judge allowed the defense. Thus, this was the first trial to extend the battered woman defense to a gay or lesbian situation.

The jury, however, did not accept the defense. Even with the complicated issues presented by the battered person defense, it took the jury only two and one-half hours to return a guilty verdict, an unusually short time. There was evidence even before the trial began that jury members had no inclination to extend the battered woman defense to a lesbian. One jury member related an incident to the judge in which two potential jurors spoke in the restroom about their desire to be

The face of homophobia: Crae Pridgen, a gay and lesbian rights activist, suffered a black eye, a badly damaged ear, and a fractured skull when he was jumped and beaten by three marines stationed at Camp Lejeune, North Carolina, in January 1993. "I was brutally beaten by people who were supposed to be protecting my rights and my freedom," Pridgen said.

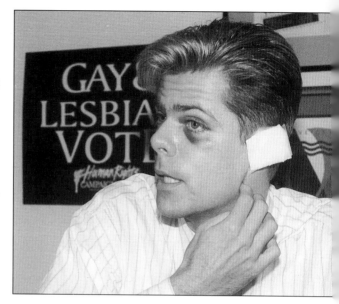

selected as jurors in order to "hang that lesbian bitch." The court personnel and guards also exhibited hostility toward the defendant. While heterosexual women also have difficulty proving a defense based upon being battered, Green's case demonstrates the problems of being a lesbian or gay criminal defendant, especially one accused of murder.

These problems also occur when the victim is not one's lover. The question is whether gays and lesbians are treated fairly within the criminal justice system when they are accused or convicted of a crime. To date, there has not been a tremendous amount of work in this area. Perhaps this is because gay and lesbian legal advocates would like to think that all lesbians, gay men, bisexuals, and transgendered persons are nice people, or even if not nice, certainly not murderers. Or perhaps this is because a focus on lesbian, gay, bisexual, and transgendered criminals is inconsistent with their other legal goals. When they are seeking abolishment of the sex statutes, an end to discrimination, and custody of their children, the negative stereotypes associated with lesbian and gay murderers can be counterproductive. Nevertheless, like every other group, some lesbians and gay men resort to violence or crime for any number of reasons.

One reason is insanity. Insanity is a well-established defense, but it is rarely successful. It may seem obvious that when someone murders a number of people, the killer may not be sane. But criminal insanity is a technical and narrow term that differs from everyday notions. It usually requires that the defendant did not know right from wrong or could not control his or her actions. Although a legal term, insanity is a question of fact rather than a question of law. This means that in a criminal trial the jury decides whether or not the defendant has established insanity. The jury is also instructed that criminal insanity means that the defendant is not criminally responsible for the actions. Although traditionally the verdict was "not guilty by reason of insanity," recently many states have revised this to "guilty but insane." In both cases, a finding of insanity usually means that the defendant is confined to an institution for the (criminally) insane. Nevertheless, the insanity defense provokes a great deal of controversy.

The widely publicized case of Jeffrey Dahmer illustrates some of the intersections between insanity, serial murder, and homosexuality. Dahmer, a white 31-year-old former chocolate-factory worker living in Milwaukee, confessed to killing 17 young men. The murders began when Dahmer was 18, continuing sporadically until 1991, a year in which he murdered at least four young men. At the time of these murders, Dahmer was on probation for a previous conviction for sexual abuse of a male child. All of Dahmer's murder victims were between the ages of 14 and 28, and most were African American, Asian, or Hispanic. Dahmer apparently lured them to his apartment with promises of a sexual experience. Once at the apartment, Dahmer drugged and murdered them. He then engaged in necrophilia, sex with a corpse. Afterwards, he performed bizarre "experiments" with the body, including cannibalism.

Dahmer pleaded guilty but insane to 15 of the murders. His 12-day trial was largely devoted to psychiatric testimony on the issue of insanity. Because Dahmer had admitted that he knew his acts were wrong (and thus that he knew the difference between right and wrong), the jury's consideration focused on Dahmer's ability to control his actions. The defense attorney argued that Dahmer suffered from a progressively worsening mental condition that made control impossible. A majority of the jury disagreed, finding Dahmer not legally insane, and he was sentenced to 15 consecutive life terms. He was later murdered in prison, allegedly by another inmate.

Whether or not one sympathizes with Dahmer, his case is relevant to this discussion because it linked homosexuality with murder. The prosecutor argued to the jury that the trial was "about a man who had sexual desires for men but didn't want it to end there. He wanted it to continue on his terms." Perhaps the prosecutor was distinguishing between a more general "desire for men" and Dahmer's "terms." But the prosecutor was also implicitly linking the two circumstances, as if a man's desire to have sex with men leads to a desire to murder them. Such links permeated the press coverage of the events. Dahmer was repeatedly referred to as a "homosexual serial killer." The media could have referred to him just as accurately as a "Milwaukee serial killer" or a "necrophiliac serial killer." The consistent choice of "homosexual" points to a troubling sort of bias.

Such bias is also evident in the case of Aileen Wuornos, known as the "lesbian serial killer." She is also known, inaccurately, as the "first female serial killer." Just as stereotypes of gay men as having uncontrollable desires are evident in Dahmer's case, stereotypes of lesbians as man-haters are evident in Wuornos's. Wuornos worked as a prostitute, often hitchhiking to attract customers. She admitted killing several male customers but argued that she did so in self-defense after they became brutally violent. In the first of her cases to come to trial, for the murder of Richard Mallory, the jury rejected Wuornos's claim of self-defense. The prosecution portrayed Mallory as an upstanding citizen and Wuornos as a dangerous man-hater. The jury convicted her of first-degree murder and recommended that she die in Florida's electric chair. The case has attracted tremendous media coverage, especially because after the trial it was learned that Mallory had spent time in prison for a violent crime against a woman.

Wuornos is not the only lesbian sentenced to death in the United States. One of the most disturbing statistics to recently come to light is that approximately 40 percent of the women on death row in the

United States may be lesbians. According to lesbian journalist Victoria Brownworth, of the 41 women sentenced to death, 17 were implicated as lesbians. Through insinuation and innuendo, prosecutors often use the defendant's lesbianism to convince the jury of the defendant's guilt. That the bias is difficult to isolate does not mean that the bias does not influence the outcomes.

There are no similar statistics concerning how many of the more than 2,500 men sentenced to death may be gay, bisexual, or transsexual. Similarly, there are no real statistics concerning the numbers of lesbians, gay men, bisexuals, and transsexuals who become involved in the criminal justice system. Once in prison, they seem to be treated differently than heterosexuals. In at least one case, a prison system initiated a policy of making lesbian prisoners wear a pink bracelet but the policy was changed after protests. It is difficult for advocates of gay and lesbian rights to protest less obvious or unarticulated policies. At times, even when they do protest policies singling out lesbians, gay men, and transsexuals, prison officials respond that the policies are necessary to "protect" such prisoners from the bias of heterosexual prisoners.

When lesbians, gay men, bisexuals, and transsexuals become involved in the criminal justice system, their sexual orientation is important. In prosecutions under the sex statutes, the importance of sexual orientation is obvious. Likewise, in prosecutions for transmitting certain diseases, sexual orientation has played a prominent role. In prosecutions for other crimes, the importance of sexual orientation may be less obvious. Sexual orientation may even be totally irrelevant to the crime. However, lesbian and gay legal advocates are beginning to struggle to ensure that sexual orientation is likewise irrelevant in the criminal justice system's response to the crime. This struggle is important whether it is the defendant, the victim, or both, who is lesbian, gay, bisexual, or transgendered.

6

⬚

Health

SINCE THE ADVENT OF AIDS with its disproportionate impact upon gay men, the intersection of health and legal issues has been of major interest to gay and lesbian legal advocates. The disease of AIDS is linked to human immunodeficiency virus (HIV), the virus that one person can transmit to another. After a latency period, the virus can result in the appearance of symptoms. Certain collections of symptoms are medically classified as AIDS.

Two men who participated in a 1983 march on Washington to heighten awareness of AIDS listen to speakers at a candlelight vigil held at the Capitol Reflecting Pool.

Medical knowledge about AIDS and HIV is developing. Since the first reported cases in 1981, the Center for Disease Control (CDC) has revised its conclusions concerning symptoms, methods of transmission, and high risk factors. This development of medical knowledge impacts upon the legal response to AIDS and HIV. For example, some of the first responses were proposals for legal quarantine of those who had the virus. States have the power to quarantine individuals because of the states' general power to promote health and safety. Despite arguments that quarantine had become an outdated option, the outbreak of AIDS renewed calls for its use against "carriers." While there have not been any wholesale quarantines, several states have enacted statutes that provide for the quarantine of "recalcitrant" HIV-infected persons. Recalcitrant is defined as persons who engage in behaviors likely to transmit HIV. States are most likely to enforce such statutes against those arrested for prostitution.

States have also struggled with the applicability of criminal law to HIV transmission. Some states have passed criminal statutes in specific response to the AIDS epidemic. These statutes generally criminalize activity by HIV-infected persons likely to transmit HIV. To be convicted under these statutes, an HIV-infected person must know her or his own HIV status and must intend to transmit the virus. Further, the prosecution must prove that the activity is one which, based upon the current state of medical knowledge, transmits HIV.

Existing crimes, such as attempted murder and assault, can also be applied to HIV transmission. Again, the defendant must know his or her HIV status and intend to transmit the virus. Prosecutions of prisoners who have bit, spit, or sprayed blood on guards or officers are the most common prosecutions in this category. However, states have also prosecuted persons arrested for prostitution, although in at least one case an appellate court found there was not sufficient intent to constitute a crime.

Transmission of HIV can also be the basis for civil suits. Such a suit could be based upon battery, negligence, or misrepresentation. As in the criminal context, however, the defendant must know he or she is HIV-positive. For example, in a suit against former basketball star Earvin "Magic" Johnson, the court rejected an argument that Johnson had a duty to warn his sexual partner that he "might" be HIV-positive because he led a "promiscuous, sexually active, and multiple partner" lifestyle.

Knowledge of HIV status requires an HIV test. Like quarantine, there have been rather dramatic proposals concerning testing, including a

In New York City in the mid-1980s, one governmental response to the heightening AIDS crisis was the closing of gay and lesbian bars, clubs, and bathhouses.

suggestion for the mandatory testing of the entire United States population. Mandatory testing is generally legally disfavored, except under the broad powers given to the Immigration and Naturalization Service to make immigration determinations. States have sought to impose mandatory testing for HIV for persons convicted of certain crimes, including prostitution and sex offenses. The general legal disfavor for mandatory testing is based upon constitutional considerations of privacy, especially as contained in the Fourth Amendment's restriction against "unreasonable searches and seizures," which is interpreted as including searching the body. In most instances a government agency cannot require an HIV test, especially as a condition for employment.

Private employers may also be limited in their ability to require an HIV test as a condition of employment. Several states have recently passed statutes that restrict HIV testing by employers in the private sector. Testing is, of course, only a manifestation of a broader legal issue. In both the private and public employment sectors as well as in housing and education, the overwhelming issue is discrimination against those who are HIV-positive or have AIDS.

While there are a few municipalities and states that have enacted laws specifically prohibiting discrimination on the basis of HIV or AIDS status, these laws are the exception rather than the rule. Generally, the

Gay and lesbian activists demonstrate for increased attention and resources for the battle against AIDS at the march commemorating the 25th anniversary of Stonewall in New York City in 1994. The Stonewall riot is regarded as the beginning of the modern gay and lesbian civil rights movement in the United States.

applicable laws are those that prohibit discrimination on the basis of handicap or disability. The two most important federal laws in this area are the Rehabilitation Act and the recently passed Americans with Disabilities Act (ADA). Also relevant are the federal Fair Housing Act and many state and local laws similar to the Rehabilitation Act and the ADA. Under these laws, a person discriminated against may be granted relief ranging from an order prohibiting the discriminatory actions to an award of money for compensatory and punitive damages. Because each law allows for different kinds of relief, often people sue under several different laws for the same discriminatory act.

The federal Rehabilitation Act of 1973 was the first important law of this sort and has served as the model for many other statutory schemes. Section 504 of the act is the central provision; it provides that no "otherwise qualified individual with handicaps . . . shall solely by reason of his or her handicap, be excluded from the participation in, be denied benefits of, or be subject to discrimination." The ADA prohibits discrimination on the basis of disability in employment, governmental programs and services, and public accommodations and services. The ADA is the latest and most comprehensive federal legislation designed to combat discrimination against those with disabilities, and it is the result of almost a decade of intense lobbying efforts by the disabled and handicapped communities. The ADA was specifically designed so it would supersede weaker laws but not prohibit any protections and remedies provided by other federal and state laws.

Even with the proliferation of laws protecting against discrimination, not all discrimination on the basis of disability or handicap is actionable. Because it is in a federal law, Section 504 applies only to programs or activities somehow connected with the federal government, including those that receive federal funds. Obviously it covers actions by federal agencies, but it also covers landlords who receive federal funding through housing programs, employers such as hospitals that receive federal funds like Medicaid or Medicare, and schools that receive federal funds for educational or loan programs. While the ADA and many state laws do not require that the organization be connected to the federal government, such laws generally exempt entities under a certain size.

For example, the ADA does not apply to employers with fewer than 15 employees.

The person who is being discriminated against must also fit under these laws. To be protected, a person must prove that he or she is handicapped or disabled. There must also be proof that the person is otherwise qualified to participate or can be so qualified with "reasonable accommodation." Each of these elements is important for persons discriminated against on the basis of AIDS or HIV infection.

AIDS and HIV infection are now considered a handicap or disability. However, not until 1987 when the United States Supreme Court decided *School Board of Nassau County v. Arline* did it became clear that a contagious disease satisfied the definitions of handicap and disability. *Arline* concerned a public elementary school teacher with contagious tuberculosis who had been fired in 1979 after a relapse of her illness. The lower courts found that someone with a contagious disease was not handicapped within the definition of the Rehabilitation Act. The appellate court reversed the decision and the Supreme Court affirmed, holding that the term "handicapped individuals" used in the act was meant to include "persons with a record of, or who are regarded as having an impairment even though they are not actually incapacitated at a particular point in time." Arline's tuberculosis has been analogized to AIDS and HIV infection. Courts now routinely consider AIDS and HIV infection to be a handicap or disability.

The requirement of "otherwise qualified" is more troublesome. In *Arline,* the Court expressly raised the question of whether someone with a contagious disease was "otherwise qualified for the job of teaching elementary school." The Court outlined factors for making such a factual determination, including the risk of transmission, the duration of the risk, and the severity of the risk. The Court specifically noted that the manner in which the disease is transmitted is relevant to determining the risk of its transmission.

The manner of transmission is especially relevant in cases of discrimination on the basis of AIDS and HIV infection. In *Chalk v. United States District Court,* a teacher in the California school system was diagnosed with AIDS and hospitalized. After returning to work, he was

The movement by gay men and lesbians to attain equal rights under the law is not, as their opponents would put it, a quest for special privileges. Instead, it is a struggle to change long-standing societal attitudes that were and are reflected in legislation and actions that function to effectively deny gay men and lesbians the full enjoyment and protection of all the rights enjoyed by other American citizens.

placed on administrative leave and later offered an administrative position at an identical salary but without student contact. He sued in federal court to challenge the school board's authority to exclude him from the classroom. The trial judge applied *Arline* but decided that the injury if transmission occurred was so great that it outweighed any injury the teacher suffered by the school reassigning him. The appellate court also applied *Arline* but found that Chalk's illness did not create an unusual risk of harm to the students. The court pointedly noted the "overwhelming evidentiary consensus of medical and scientific opinion regarding the nature and transmission of AIDS" and observed that studies have consistently found no apparent risk of HIV infection to individuals exposed through close nonsexual contact.

The perception that a person has AIDS or HIV infection can also be a source of discrimination. Such perceptions intersect with discrimination on the basis of sexual orientation, especially in the case of gay men. For example, Rod Miller went to the emergency room with a severed tendon in his foot. At the hospital, doctors informed him that he needed immediate surgery to prevent permanent injury. As Miller was being prepared for surgery, some of the hospital staff informed the surgeon, Dr. Spicer, that Miller was gay. The staff communicated this information by making derogatory statements and snide remarks about Miller and his companions. Dr. Spicer examined Miller in what Miller called a very rough and brusque manner and demanded to know Miller's HIV status. Miller stated that while he had been tested, the outcome of his test was not known. Dr. Spicer then told Miller that because there were no test results, he would not perform the necessary surgery on Miller. Miller transferred to another hospital, but because of the time that had elapsed, he was left permanently injured.

In such a situation, several laws might apply. Federal laws preventing discrimination on the basis of handicap or disability applied to the hospital because it received federal funds and had many employees but did not apply to Dr. Spicer as an individual. Miller therefore sued Dr. Spicer for intentional infliction of emotional distress, a theory of personal injury law. Additionally, a recent federal law and many similar state laws specifically require hospitals to provide emergency medical care to all patients with emergency medical conditions.

The availability of health care is a vital issue for persons with AIDS or HIV infection. Although much of the work for lawyers concerned with AIDS issues involves litigating individual cases such as Miller's, the bulk of it consists of lobbying federal, state, and local governments and agencies concerning AIDS and HIV treatments and research. Decisions concerning whether a new drug should be used on a trial basis, who should receive that drug, and who should be responsible for determining its effectiveness are not decisions merely for medical experts. Such decisions involve broad social issues. Legal representation of those being affected by medical policy decisions has become extremely important.

Gay and lesbian advocates are concerned with other medical issues as well. For lesbians, an important issue has been exclusion from medical research. Such an exclusion may occur because women are generally excluded from medical research, except when the research specifically concerns reproductive capacities. But even when women are included, lesbians may not be. For example, the National Institute for Health, a federal agency, recently authorized the largest study of women's health issues in history. Predictably, the study omitted any attention to sexual orientation. Lawyers intervened, lobbying the agency to include sexual orientation in the study. Such an inclusion may mean that conditions which disproportionately affect lesbians could be identified before the outbreak of an epidemic.

Current national debates concerning health care also involve issues particular to lesbians, gay men, bisexuals, and transgendered persons. Public policy decisions concerning what conditions and treatments should be covered by any national health insurance system may have differing impacts depending on sexual orientation. Further, definitions of "next of kin" or "family" are also important, especially since such definitions might determine who will be responsible for medical expenses or decisions. Lawyers from the lesbian and gay legal community—acting not in the traditional role of courtroom litigators but as public policy advocates—are attempting to have a positive effect on the multitude of health concerns of lesbians, gay men, bisexuals, and transgendered persons.

7

The Legal
Profession

*Participants gather on the
Mall in front of the Capitol
in Washington, D.C.,
as part of the March on
Washington for Lesbian
and Gay Rights in April
1993. With an estimated
one million participants, the
march was the culmination
thus far of the movement
for equal rights for lesbians
and gays.*

MANY GAY MEN AND lesbians have worked in the legal profession as judges, attorneys, paralegals, and legal secretaries. However, it is only in recent years that gay men and lesbians working in the legal profession have been able to be open about their sexual identities. For legal secretaries and paralegals, employment discrimination on the basis of sexual orientation was common. For attorneys and judges, professional rules requiring "good moral character" operated to exclude sexual minorities.

The situation of Harris Kimball illustrates some of the recent changes for gay men and lesbians in the legal profession. The Florida bar admitted Kimball in 1953.

The usual process of admission consists of passing a bar examination and meeting the character requirements, after which the applicant is licensed as an attorney. Duly licensed, Kimball began to practice law. The police arrested him two years later for engaging in oral sex with another man on a local beach, charging him with violating a city sex ordinance. The Florida bar learned of this incident and sought to revoke his license to

practice law. This process of disbarment included a lengthy hearing at which Kimball, the other man, and the police officers testified. Despite Kimball's denials, the finding was that he had committed an act "contrary to good morals and the laws of the state." Kimball was disbarred. Eighteen years later, he again attempted to become a licensed attorney. By this time, he had moved to New York and had become

An organization representing the lesbian and gay law students of New York University was among those that demonstrated in favor of New York City's Gay Rights Bill in March 1986. In recent years, gay men and lesbians have become much more visible in the legal community.

involved in gay and lesbian liberation struggles. After passing the New York bar examination, Kimball faced the Committee on Character and Fitness with two problems. First, he was an "admitted homosexual" who also admitted to engaging in "homosexual acts"; New York had never before explicitly certified such a person to practice law. Second, he had previously been disbarred in another state; New York, like most states, disapproves of such a person without unusual circumstances. The Committee on Character and Fitness referred the case to an appellate court, which decided that Kimball should be denied admission. Kimball appealed to New York's highest court, which reversed the lower court's decision. He was granted admission to the New York bar in 1973.

Kimball's case is an important milestone for gay and lesbian attorneys. Other states have since adopted the New York position. For example, Florida—where Kimball was originally disbarred—disbarred another attorney for similar acts in 1970 but indicated that the disbarment was only temporary and later readmitted him. In 1978, the Supreme Court of Florida decided that an applicant of "homosexual orientation" satisfied the good moral character qualification of the bar. The Florida court at this time specifically delayed the question of whether "homosexual acts" as well as "orientation" could satisfy the good moral character requirement. A few years later, in 1981, the Florida court was faced with a situation in which a gay applicant for admission to the bar was being asked questions about his sexual conduct. The court held that "private noncommercial sex acts between consenting adults are not relevant to prove the fitness to practice law." Although in all of these cases some justices of the court disagreed, the rules for bar admission are now generally interpreted as not excluding applicants on the basis of sexual orientation or private sexual conduct.

In the case of lesbians and bisexual women, the historical exclusion of women from the legal profession is also relevant. Although women have been welcomed within the ranks of supporting workers who do most of the work for a fraction of the pay, women were routinely excluded from being paralegals, court reporters, or lawyers. Historically, only a few states allowed women to practice law. In 1872, the United

States Supreme Court denied a challenge by Mrs. Bradwell to Illinois's exclusion of her from the practice of law on the basis of her gender. The Court stated that the "paramount destiny and mission of women are to fulfil the noble and benign offices of wife and mother. This is the law of the Creator." This attitude that women should be wives and mothers rather than attorneys prevailed for almost a century. Until the late 1960s, most state bars, state law schools, and private law schools had a policy of excluding women, an exclusion that resulted in 97–98 percent of all attorneys being male. Of the few female attorneys, only about 25 in the nation were women of color. While there are no statistics about the number of lesbians who were attorneys in this period, the number is probably minimal because there were so few female attorneys. Being openly lesbian within this group would have been even rarer. If women attorneys were an "invisible bar," as one historian claims, then lesbian attorneys were invisible even within that invisible bar.

Yet lesbian attorneys existed. For example, Anyda Marchant attended National Law School, a private law school that admitted women, on a scholarship funded by the Women's Bar Association of the District of Columbia. After graduating in 1936, she practiced with a small firm and then worked at the Law Library of Congress during World War II. When the male attorney whose position she had filled returned from soldiering, she lost her job. Over the next several decades, she practiced law in an international context, with positions in Brazil, in a large firm, and for agencies of the United States government. She also maintained a committed relationship with her companion, Muriel, starting in 1948. When she retired from the law in 1972, she devoted herself to writing fiction and continues to publish novels under her pen name, Sarah Aldridge.

Marchant and Kimball both weathered difficult times as attorneys. It is difficult to know how many other lesbian, gay, bisexual, or transgendered persons survived in the overwhelmingly heterosexual, male, white, and conservative atmosphere of the legal profession in the United States that prevailed until the 1970s. The history of these pioneering legal workers remains largely unknown.

Today there are many openly gay, lesbian, and bisexual attorneys and other legal workers. It is nevertheless difficult to discuss a typical one. I have met many—probably hundreds—of lesbian, gay, bisexual, and transgendered legal workers during my own legal career, which has included working for two federal judges, practicing law on behalf of poor persons with a legal services organization, and teaching others to enter the legal profession. Some of these legal workers have been open about their sexuality and some have not; some have made career choices connected to their sexuality and some have made career choices completely independent of their sexuality.

The most well known lesbian, gay, bisexual, and transgendered legal workers are those who have devoted their legal careers to advocacy on behalf of lesbian, gay, bisexual and transgendered persons. In many instances, this devotion has meant less pay and less prestige than those who have pursued more traditional career paths. Many of these legal workers are associated with one of several national legal organizations in the United States that work for lesbian, gay, bisexual, and trans-gendered rights, including the Lambda Legal Defense and Education Fund, the National Center for Lesbian Rights, the National Lesbian and Gay Task Force, and the Campaign for Human Rights. Additionally, there are many local and state organizations that do advocacy and litigation on behalf of gay rights. There are also special gay and lesbian sections of national organizations such as the American Civil Liberties Union (ACLU) and the National Lawyers Guild. In addition to employing attorneys and other legal workers, these organizations also "associate" with many lesbian and gay legal workers in private practice. Private attorneys often donate their time and resources, working pro bono on specific cases. At times, these cases achieve national attention and make new law. In many instances, however, these cases are small contributions to a gradual shift in the law or are important only to the individual lesbian, gay, bisexual, or transgendered clients.

Another network consists of specific lesbian and gay legal workers' associations. The largest is the National Lesbian and Gay Law Association, which sponsors the important "Lavender Law" conference. This conference occurs every other year, rotating through regions of the

*This placard displayed by an observer of New York City's annual
Gay Pride Parade expresses a sentiment with which, in all likelihood,
all those who have worked to reform the law so that it provides fairer
treatment for lesbians and gay men would agree.*

country, and serves as a teaching and learning experience for advocates working on all aspects of lesbian and gay legal issues. Regional lesbian and gay law associations, such as Bay Area Lawyers for Individual Freedom (BALIF) in San Francisco also sponsor conferences on legal issues for lesbians and gay men. At such conferences, legal advocates share information, discuss strategies, and develop expertise in different areas of the law.

Lesbians, gay men, bisexuals, and transgendered persons associated with law schools have also developed networks. The American Association of Law Schools has a section for gay and lesbian law professors, which presents programs at the law professors' annual conference and takes positions regarding policies affecting legal education. At many law schools, there are student organizations for lesbian, gay, bisexual, and transgendered law students. These organizations often sponsor speakers, participate in conferences, protest discriminatory campus policies, recruit potential law school applicants, and serve as a social center.

There are also groups of paralegals, judges, law librarians, and legal secretaries, all of which advocate for gay and lesbian rights within their respective professional circles. All these associations, including those for attorneys, law professors, and students, provide support for legal workers and prevent them from becoming isolated. Further, these organizations support the cause of lesbian and gay civil rights through their legal work.

There are also many lesbian, gay, bisexual, and transgendered legal workers who do not join associations and are not involved in advocacy on behalf of civil rights. These legal workers may or may not be open about their sexuality. They may be judges, paralegals, legal secretaries, or attorneys involved in any one of the numerous areas of law not consistently relevant to lesbian, gay, bisexual, and transgendered issues: patents and trademarks, income tax, corporate finance, securities, personal injury, public benefits, and real property. Yet every area of law potentially affects gay men and lesbians. And every legal worker who is lesbian, gay, bisexual, or transgendered has a potential impact both on the legal profession and upon the law.

There is tremendous disagreement within the lesbian and gay legal community about what this impact should be. Some believe that the simple existence of openly lesbian, gay, bisexual, and transgendered legal professionals will change the profession and the law for the better by making it more tolerant of sexual diversity. Others believe that the role of lesbian, gay, bisexual, and transgendered legal professionals should be to fundamentally challenge the legal system, rather than becoming comfortable within it. Only the future will reveal which path the lesbian, gay, bisexual, and transgendered legal community will pursue.

▣ *Further Reading* ▣

Leonard, Arthur S. *Sexuality and the Law: An Encyclopedia of Major Cases*. New York: Garland Publishing, 1993.

Robson, Ruthann. *Lesbian (Out)Law: Survival Under the Rule of Law*. Ithaca, NY: Firebrand Books, 1992.

Rubenstein, William, ed. *Lesbians, Gay Men, and the Law*. New York: The New Press, 1993.

PICTURE CREDITS

◙ *Index* ◙

Ruthann Robson is professor of law at the City University of New York School of Law, where she teaches in the areas of constitutional law, criminal procedure, family law, sexuality and the law, feminist legal theory, and administrative law. After graduating from law school in 1979, she clerked for two federal judges and then practiced law for several years for a poverty law organization. In addition to being the author of *Lesbian (Out)Law: Survival Under the Rule of Law*, she is the author of two acclaimed collections of lesbian short fiction, *Cecile* and *Eye of a Hurricane*, and a novel, *Another Mother*, about a lesbian attorney.

Martin Duberman is Distinguished Professor of History at the Graduate Center for the City University of New York and the founder and director of the Center for Lesbian and Gay Studies. One of the country's foremost historians, he is the author of 17 books and numerous articles and essays. He has won the Bancroft Prize for *Charles Francis Adams* (1960); two Lambda awards for *Hidden from History: Reclaiming the Gay and Lesbian Past*, an anthology that he coedited; and a special award from the National Academy of Arts and Letters for his overall "contributions to literature." His play *In White America* won the Vernon Rice/Drama Desk Award in 1964. His other works include *James Russell Lowell* (1966), *Black Mountain: An Exploration in Community* (1972), *Paul Robeson* (1989), *Cures: A Gay Man's Odyssey* (1991), *Stonewall* (1993), *Midlife Queer* (1996), and *A Queer World* (1996).